IRMA BRINGS LOVE

MAUREEN A. PETERS

ISBN 978-1-64416-286-6 (paperback)
ISBN 978-1-64416-287-3 (digital)

Christian Faith Publishing, Inc.
832 Park Avenue
Meadville, PA 16335
www.christianfaithpublishing.com

Printed in the United States of America

This book is dedicated to my family and all British Virgin Islands citizens and residents whose love for their country and home gave them the courage to be a part of the process of rebuilding after the passing of category 5 Hurricane Irma on September 6, 2017.

INTRODUCTION

On September 6, 2017, the tropical Caribbean islands of the British Virgin Islands changed forever.

Nature's Little Secrets, as the British Virgin Islands (BVI) is called, has just under thirty thousand residents. Many residents and visitors lived through some unforgettable natural disasters during 2017.

The BVI which is located sixty miles east of Puerto Rico is comprised of approximately sixty islands, islets, and cays, with Tortola being the largest. It boasts clean, clear waters, miles of picturesque white sand beaches and has been dubbed "the sailing capital of the world."

Virgin Gorda, the second most populated, is home to "The Baths," a natural formation of large rock boulders that provides for great hiking adventure, swimming, and snorkeling.

Jost Van Dyke is home to the famous Foxy's Beach Bar, which is located on one of its beautiful beaches and is owned and operated by musical entertainer—Foxy Callwood. Foxy possesses the unique ability of creating a song on the spot as the scenes unfold.

Anegada, which is quite an adventure to travel to, boasts an array of seafood. The annual Lobster Fest draws residents and visitors to the succulent seafood dishes available by the various beach bar restaurants. To dive the Wreck of the Rhone, just off Anegada, will make a memorable experience for any dive enthusiast.

Visitors travel for miles to enjoy the beauty of Nature's Little Secrets, something that many residents fail to do, and sometimes even fail to see. However, on the morning of August 8, the surrounding beauty was altered by a flood, which left unbelievable damage to the infrastructure of the territory.

Then on September 6, when many residents and visitors alike thought that the earth could take no more water or any further damage after the flood, Hurricane Irma passed by packing category 5 strength winds and changed everyone's life forever.

Many persons have reported having to run during the active parts of the hurricane from where they felt safe to a safer place, some even having to leave the "new" place of safety.

Each person was left with a story to tell. Those who were not running for a safer shelter were fighting with a door or some other item, and some were injured.

Nevertheless, *Irma Brings Love* aims to show that good can be found in the midst of disaster.

CHAPTER 1

Tianna jumped.

For some reason, her cell phone just sounded louder than usual.

She was at the restaurant where she worked in the office a couple days a week. It was one of her income-producing ventures, the only one closest to a nine-to-five job. She actually preferred not to get caught up in it. However, this arrangement worked for her as the manager allowed her to be flexible with her time. The only requirement was that she be informed ahead of time. Tianna was free to be as creative as she liked with the filing, the creation of documents and forms, and the Facebook posts. She truly enjoyed this assignment on the days that she was there.

At one point, she had felt attacked by family members about not having a *real* job. Their heads were obviously stuck in the slave-master age, Tianna always thought to herself. Her work schedule afforded her the privilege to do exactly what she wanted. On Mondays she would map out her schedule for the week. This would be preceded by a run, or a massage session, or a swim at one of the nearby beaches. She did not earn as much as she wanted, but she never had to ask anyone for money. This arrangement gave her great peace of mind. She had made up her mind to sacrifice certain comforts so that she could have the kind of life she wanted.

When she arrived at the office, there were paper and files everywhere. She took a few minutes to sort them and created a clear working space. Then after responding to the few e-mails in the inbox, she started finalizing the month-end reports.

"Hello," she said, trying to sound focused.

"You sound like you were sleeping," the voice called back.

"I wish I were. These numbers are driving me crazy," she sighed.

It was Semajj.

When Tianna had the opportunity to work in the technical ministry of her home church, Semajj was one of the persons she met. Over the years many persons passed through the ministry. Yet almost ten years later, they both remained, and were consistent in their service. Tianna had learned a lot about the variety of technical operations and ensured that she passed on her knowledge to those who joined the ministry after her.

Semajj was employed at a hardware store and thus met many persons. He was very knowledgeable and helpful. Tianna had been to that hardware store several times and benefitted from his kind assistance. If she said she wanted a one-inch pipe, he would ask her all the pertinent questions to ensure that she left with exactly what she wanted—what length, water or electrical. She had high regard for the service he provided whenever she would visit the store to make a purchase.

"Anyway," he said, "hold on for me."

"Hello," a different voice came on.

"Yes," she answered.

"Is this the lady that owns the small yellow house?" he questioned.

"Yes, I own the small yellow wooden house."

"My brother is interested in renting it. When can we take a look at it?"

"I still have some work to do on it."

"That's okay. When is a good time for you to show it?"

"Will this afternoon at five-thirty be good?"

The phone went blank for a moment while Tianna listened as the voice on the other end repeated her question to someone in the background.

"Okay! That sounds good," he said when he got back to the phone.

"All right then, I'll see you at the house."

The conversation ended, and Tianna went back to working on the month-end reports that had her in deep concentration when the phone rang. It was her desire to mark this assignment complete before she left for the day.

It was Valentine's Day, and she looked forward to pampering herself later that evening as she had no one to spend it with.

Later that day, when Tianna checked the time, she could not believe it was five o'clock already. She hurriedly finished up what she was doing so that she could get home to the appointment.

In the past days, a number of persons had taken interest in the little yellow house she had built on a section of her property. It was built at a time when her main house was rented, and she had nowhere else to live. While asking the tenants to leave could have been an option, she knew at the time that her salary could not sustain her and pay the mortgage.

Though the house was only two hundred and eighty-eight square feet, Tianna had found the tiny house to be a place of great comfort and solace, even without the basic comforts of electricity, running water, and toilet facilities.

A single mother with a teenage son was desperately interested in the house. Even ahead of her required time frame, she wanted to put her personal belongings in the house.

Another interested person was a gentleman who also wanted the house upgrades to be sorted out within his desired timeframe.

Their time frames were not within Tianna's convenience.

Tianna arrived at the house before anyone else. She had completed the month-end reports and presented them to her boss for submission the following day. This put her mind at ease.

As she entered the house, a feeling of solace came over her. This house occupied a very special place in her heart, as she always liked wooden houses. She often dreamed of having one of her own. There were two bedrooms that were the perfect size for her twin beds. Each room had a window with an ocean view that brought breeze into the house and kept the entire house cool. The bathroom just enough for one person, and the kitchen was the focal point when entering the house. Although she never liked a house where visitors entered the kitchen first, the cabinets in this kitchen were so nice that she became comfortable with the arrangement.

It was a hard decision for her to move to the main house, but this did not stop her from spending time in the wooden house on some evenings.

She heard a vehicle drive into the yard and slowly made her way to the front door, still making notes. She stopped dead in her tracks when a handsome young man appeared in the doorway.

He wore what looked like a hat that is worn by cricket players. It was lowered on his face so that it was almost covering his thick eyebrows and gleaming eyes. The muscles in his arms were so clearly defined they looked like he worked in a gym. He wore a close fit T-shirt and blue jeans with a pair of brown boots.

Neither said a word. They just starred at each other.

The silence was soon interrupted, though, by the thunderous steps of a beautiful full-figured young lady. Her makeup was flawless. It matched the turquoise sweater-jacket that she wore. This covered a printed inner blouse with turquoise, white, and black, and a black skirt. Her feet looked picture perfect in the flat shiny black shoes she wore.

"Hi," she said with an energy of authoritarianism.

Tianna then found her voice. She turned to the young man and asked, "Was it you that called me today?"

Before he could say anything, the young lady declared, "That was my husband. This is my brother-in-law. We live next door."

Pointing to the young man, she announced, "He is interested in renting your house."

She reached out her hand for a handshake. The young man did the same.

"I'm Shadè Payne, and this is Joshua," she pointed out.

"Tianna Corrington, nice to meet you both."

Shadè started talking about the price, while Joshua looked around.

"Well, like I told your husband, there is still some work to be done. I have lived in it like this, but it is not ideal for everyone," Tianna reiterated.

"What all needs to be done?" Shadè asked.

"The plumbing is not complete. The toilet is in place, but it is not connected to the septic. The water connection to the house and the electrical works need to be done."

"Will you be willing to reduce the monthly rent if he agrees to take the place, *as is*, and fix it up?"

After pausing for a few seconds, Tianna agreed.

It was only then that Shadè invited Joshua into the conversation by asking him what he thought about the proposal.

Joshua agreed to the arrangement Shadè proposed. He then asked a few questions of his own about making some adjustments to the layout of the house.

"Whatever makes you happy," was all Tianna said in response as she was so happy to finally have the house generating income. She felt it in her gut that Joshua would take care of the place as if it were his own. Her heart's desire was that whoever rented the house would take care of it as if it were their own.

Tianna agreed to e-mail the contract to Shadè for review, and they said their goodbyes.

It was a beautiful moonlit evening, and Tianna was alone, spending Valentine's Day by herself—another year. She made up her mind that she would treat herself to a homemade dinner this year.

Her appetizer was the remaining *ginger pumpkin soup* that she loved so much but had made for the first time the Sunday before. It tasted so good that she froze some just for this moment, and it was perfect.

She made a vegetarian lasagna for her dinner, not because she was vegetarian but because she loved to cook, and with each dish, she expected to learn something new or different. Besides, lasagna was one of her favorite food. Having made other versions, she decided to make one without meat. No meal, of course, was complete without some fried overripe plantain and coleslaw with raisins, according to Tianna.

For dessert she made a zucchini cake. The method she used was so quick and easy. She sliced and blended three zucchini with three eggs and three-quart vegetable oil. That mixture was poured into a large bowl of two cups sifted flour, one and a half cups sugar, one tablespoon baking powder, and some cinnamon, allspice, and ground nutmeg. After mixing well, she poured the batter in a circular baking pan that allow for a hole in the center of her cake. There was no end to how creative she could be in decorating her cake, but she chose to just line the top of it with halved cherries.

The small circular table on her covered back porch was elegantly adorned with a red tablecloth, which was trimmed with a floral-patterned black-and-white runner. Red napkins were folded in a fan shape and resting on the plain white plate. The silverware were glistening with the light from the clear sky above. She did not need to turn on any light in the house.

Tianna felt so good about this special treatment when she finally sat down to eat, dressed in her off-shoulder ankle-length romper and silver accessories.

"Wow!" she said as she poured herself a glass of white grape Chamdor. "This looks so lovely, and the food is so nice. It is a shame to not share it with someone."

Five years ago, this would have been unheard of. She had spent several years of her life in a close relationship with Lance. She thought he was everything she ever wanted in a man—except that he was short. Apart from that, he was a perfect gentleman.

Lance always remembered every special occasion. He could even recall what she considered small and insignificant details, like when and where they first met and their first dinner out. He took special care to ensure that she was always happy. That's why she remembered him on a night like tonight. He went as far as to write a song for her about the moonlight, yet that was not to be.

It is Joshua Payne, however, that she now desired to sit with her under the moonlight. They had met for the first time a few hours before, but her heart was still palpitating at the thought of looking into his bright eyes and being held by his strong arms.

It had been quite a while since she had such thoughts.

Joshua spent much of his time alone. He enjoyed nature so much that he could be found outside on the porch or in some comfortable spot watching the stars or the moon on a moonlit night. He always wondered why his teachers all seemed to feel that he was too quiet when he did not feel that way about himself.

When doing assignments, especially when it came to being creative, like in art class or when he was learning carpentry, his personal space meant the world to him. He paid great attention to detail whenever he was committed to a project that sparked his interest. For him, an excellent outcome was the only acceptable outcome. His woodwork projects were always neat, and he always kept his surrounding tidy.

Although he was not one to get all worked up about what most people would consider special days, like birthdays and Valentine's Day, the memories of this Valentine's Day would forever be encapsulated in his mind.

Joshua only knew it was Valentine's Day because most of the guys on the job were making a big fuss about making dinner plans or getting something nice for their wife or girlfriend. Those who were not constantly on the phone for most of the day took an extended lunch period.

Thoughts of Tianna were bombarding his mind since their meeting at her wooden house. She seemed so kind and loving, he thought. He was particularly fascinated with the fact that she gave him permission to make himself comfortable in her house by adjusting it to his liking.

"Wow!" he whispered to himself. "I can't say I was actively looking for a wife, but I have found exactly what I want. It just feels so right."

He lay on his bed and dozed off in quiet thoughts of Tianna, his new landlady.

CHAPTER

This was turning out to be Tianna's favorite day of the year, after her birthday and Christmas. Every birthday deserved a big celebration according to her. It was a day that signified abundant blessings, as she felt that life was too precious not to enjoy.

For her, Christmas was indeed the most wonderful time of the year. Each year her family had a sleepover. They would gather at a designated home on Christmas Eve and spend all night eating, singing, playing games, and laughing. They created their own games to make sure that every family member could participate.

She had long desired to have this little place rented. So much work had gone into making it attractive and livable for renters. She had inside panel walls added and painted them, along with other little projects. Yet there was still so much to do.

While Tianna's mind was always consumed with all that had to be done to make the house more comfortable, today her thoughts were different.

"Oh my goodness, what is wrong with me?" Tianna sighed heavily.

"Lord, your word says in Isaiah 26:3 that thou would keep them in perfect peace, whose minds are stayed on thee. Grant me some peace of mind right now," she prayed.

"Why is Joshua just consuming my thoughts? I need to pull myself together before he gets here to sign this contract. Anyway, Ms. Shadè will be there," she said to herself as she wriggled her head.

Just then her eyes caught a glimpse of motion.

"Is that her?" Tianna wondered as she observed a female figure walking in her direction.

When she got a clear view, she put on a smile and got out of the car and greeted her warmly.

"Hi, Shadè, how was your day?"

"Hectic, but good."

"How was yours?"

"Wonderful!"

"Hope I did not keep you waiting too long."

Tianna looked at her watch. The twenty minutes she was sitting there seemed to have gone by so swiftly.

"No worries," she replied. It was one of the sayings she picked up during her trip to a martial arts tournament in Melbourne, Australia. She thoroughly enjoyed the trip. Although she had not participated in any of the events, she supported the other team members. Team BVI (British Virgin Islands) of which she was a part comprised of five persons including her.

Team BVI returned home with a few medals. They were received at the airport with a grand welcome by the team members who did not make the trip. A meeting was later set to watch the videos and pictures that Tianna and others had taken.

There were teams from Canada, Cayman Islands, Antigua, and Trinidad and Tobago. The group was made up of over twenty-five persons.

"Sorry to be late," the male voice seemed to roar from behind the ladies. It made them both jump as neither saw him approaching.

Joshua had left work a little earlier to get to the meeting on time. This meant that he had to walk home from Beef Island. He hoped to get a ride, but none was going his way. When he arrived, the ladies were already there.

"You frightened me," they said in unison.

"Sorry about that, it was not my intention. Have you signed the contract yet?"

"No," Shadè answered, "we were waiting for you to get here."

"Well, I'm here. Let's do this thing."

The three of them walked to the house. Tianna opened the door and used the kitchen counter as a desk, and each person signed, with Shadè as witness to Joshua's signature.

Shadè gave Tianna a check for the first month's rent, and Tianna handed over the keys. They had agreed to forgo the deposit in exchange for the works to be done by Joshua.

After Tianna handed over the receipt, they went their separate ways.

Joshua tossed and turned in his bed. He could not sleep, as he could not take his mind off his new landlady. Yes, she seemed a bit more mature than many of the ladies that looked her age, but he found himself falling for her more and more with every interaction.

She wore no makeup, yet her face was such a smooth, even dark chocolate tone, and her skin always seemed to glow. She smiled so radiantly it made him want to stop and stare. Her attire was like that of a lawyer. She always wore black, sometimes a dress and other times a suit.

Why is one of her eyes different from the other? he wondered. *I will ask her the next time I see her.*

I wonder where she works, he pondered.

Joshua rolled over on his queen-sized bed and sighed.

"I would really like to get to know her better. I wonder if she's married. I'll check out her finger the next time I see her, and if there is none, I will ask her," he planned.

He continued deep in thought until he fell asleep.

A month later, there was a knock at Tianna's door. She paused. Wrinkles appeared across her forehead as she wondered who it might be, because she did not hear a vehicle drive into the yard.

Then she heard the knock again.

"Oh, it might be Joshua," she whispered. The butterflies in her stomach started dancing nervously with excitement.

The rent was due. She had already written a receipt but left the date blank.

"Coming," she hollered as she grabbed the rose-pink bathrobe her mom had given her. It was only to cover the wrap she was wearing.

She always felt so comfortable in wraps while at home as they kept her cool and were great to just slip on and off when she was working on a new outfit.

Sewing was one of Tianna's favorite pastimes. She and her sisters had started making clothes for their dolls long before their mom would allow them to use a needle and thread. They would cut out the pattern for the doll's outfit and put it together with tape.

Tianna's mother, Izzy, as her dad called her, was a very good seamstress who made clothing for many of the neighbors. One year she received an award for making the cheerleaders' sports day uniform for Tianna's school. Although Tianna never took part in sports, she was always supportive of her sister, Jan, who mastered the long-distance races. Jan's strategy was unorthodox. She would put all her energy into the first part of the race. As she made her way around the track, scores of people could be heard telling her to slow down or she would burn out. She would keep going until she would burn out at the finish line, long before everyone else. It worked every time to secure her a first place medal.

Tianna peeped through the window, and a big smile automatically covered her face. She took a deep breath and opened the door.

"Hi, how are you?" she said, trying to act normal, knowing that nothing about how she felt was normal in Joshua's presence.

"I'm okay. I came to pay the rent."

After counting the cash he gave her, Tianna slipped it into one pocket. She retrieved the receipt book and pen from the other pocket of the robe and inputted the date. She then tore the page out and gave Joshua his copy.

"Thanks! Ah, when will the electrician come by to put the outlet in the kitchen and do the other works?" Joshua asked as he looked at the receipt.

"I called him several times this week, and he just put me off, but I will touch base with him again and let you know when."

"Okay, no problem."

For Tianna it was a problem. Her number one interest was to make Joshua, or anyone who crossed her path, as comfortable as possible. Now here she was being put in a spot to make excuse after excuse. If she could do the electrical work herself, she would have just done it.

Tianna was not afraid of hard work, or any work for that matter. All she needed was good instructions, and she was on the job.

During the construction of her main house, she got physically involved so that she could learn as much as she could. The only things she did not do were lay blocks, plaster the walls, and carpentry work. As a matter of fact, she had tiled the entire bathroom of the house Joshua was renting, and her son had helped her bend and tie the steel for the septic. When her friend stopped by to help with the septic, all he had to do was deck it and pour the concrete. He could not believe she and her young son had done such an impressive steelwork. It was not perfect, but it was done better than a lot of persons in the field, he had commented.

Their work turned out to be a blessing not just to them but to their new tenant.

CHAPTER 3

Joshua could always count on his best friend, Kaii, for an honest opinion on whatever he faced. They had been friends since child-hood. They even shared the same birth month, with birthdays a day apart.

The two learned carpentry at the same time and were both con-sidered the best wherever they went to work. They took such pride in their work that their employers would talk about how fascinating it was to secretly watch them work. In addition, they always left their work areas clean and tidy.

Although Joshua was still trying to determine the right time to tell Kaii about Tianna, Kaii could read him like a book.

One day as Joshua and Kaii were having lunch, Kaii noticed there was a change in his best friend's countenance.

"Man, what's wrong with you? You seem so quiet these days," Kaii inquired.

"Nothing, man! I'm just thinking."

"Thinking about what?"

"Nothing! You know I'm always quiet."

"Nah, not like that. Something's on your mind. You're not even eating your lunch. Look at you."

"Okay! Remember the new place I told you about? The house I got for rent?"

"Yeah, what happened? They're not renting it to you again?"

"No."

"So you have to find someplace else?"

"No, it's not that."

"Then what?"

"It's the landlady."

"The landlady?"

Joshua took a deep breath.

"Dude, you have a crush on your landlady? Ha, I never thought I would see the day," Kaii teased.

"So you're laughing at me?"

"No, dude, I'm happy for you. But the landlady? She has to be a really fine chick." Kaii rubbed his chin. "Let's see." He paused and looked up. "She at least has a house which you live in."

"I think it's two."

"What?"

"Yes. I think so because the houses are on the same piece of land, so I think she owns them both."

"Even better! The sister probably has some cheddar stashed away. Hey, you'll have to hook up your boy," Kaii said as he rubbed his hands together.

"Man, you know I'm not into all that."

"So tell me, what about this landlady," he continued to tease.

"She's different. She's pleasant, has a heart to help others. She's positive and just seems to have it together," Joshua rattled off as if he was presenting a report for which he was proud.

"Sounds like you've been really paying attention to this landlady person. So what's her name?"

If he had been asked this question before he'd paid his rent recently, he would not have been able to answer. However, when he received his last rent receipt, he paid attention to the name on the signature because he had not even heard her say her name at their initial introduction, nor did he read the contract.

"Tianna. Tianna Corr—something or the other. I can't really remember the last name."

"Listen, the name does not matter. My question is, what's really bothering you?" Kaii asked with a disconcerted look on his face.

"Well, she seems a little more mature, and she might figure I'm not good enough for her since I don't have an office job." He paused. "Maybe she's seeing someone."

"Have you ever seen her with anyone?"

"No, but it might be that he's away and I'm just wasting my time like with Mandy."

"Yeah, I remember Mandy in high school. She was definitely not for you. As a matter of fact, when she hurt you so bad, I thought that you would be a bachelor for the rest of your life. Now here comes tequila."

Joshua laughed.

"Man, you drink too much. It's Tianna."

"Yeah, whatever. Look, all I know is that mature or mature not, if your heart is in it, you should follow your heart."

"Kaii," the foreman called as soon as the last word came out of his mouth.

"Sir," he answered.

"See me when you have a minute."

Kaii raised his hand as his response and turned his attention back to Joshua.

"On a serious note, man, this might be your chance to find love again. Don't let it slip away."

With that, Kaii walked off and headed to the foreman's office.

Joshua was truly happy in his little house. His landlady told him to make himself comfortable, and that is what he was determined to do. He always liked wooden houses.

Tianna had agreed to get her electrician to install the missing outlet in the kitchen. When he came by to see exactly what needed to be done and what material she would need to purchase, Tianna had an opportunity to observe the changes Joshua had made in the few months he was living there.

Her first observation was that the floor was covered. It looked like it was painted in an earth-tone color that stood out beautifully against the white walls. Tianna had started painting the walls white but never completed the job. However, the finished work that Joshua had done on the walls made the house look so homey.

Joshua had even painted inside the kitchen cabinets white. They looked so nice and clean that Tianna decided in her mind that she would paint the cabinets in the main house white on the inside.

The partition between the two bedrooms was removed to create a spacious one bedroom that allowed for generous breeze into the space. The queen-sized bed was nicely made up and positioned in one corner of the room.

Prior to renting the house to Joshua, Tianna had spent many hours trying to figure out how to position the fridge away from the front door. She eventually gave up on the idea with the thought that whoever moved in would decide for themselves. Well, Joshua had positioned his fridge in an area that she would not have thought of. He abandoned the use of one of the doors to the bedroom and placed the fridge in front of it. This, however, meant that an outlet would have to be installed, but it allowed for more space in the kitchen.

After seeing the house that day, Tianna was very comfortable with her decision to rent the house to Joshua.

With Tianna's permission, Joshua constructed a clothesline at the back of the house. There were days when he would see her on her back porch hanging out clothes while he himself was putting clothes on his line. At those times he would just put himself in a position where he could just admire her.

It was mostly on a Sunday afternoon that he would see her. She always seemed to be in a good mood, singing a song. Her attire was always the same—a wrap. It seemed that she liked them so much she always had a different one on. That was a good thing, though, because the way they hugged her body made her look like a model.

Watching her reminded him of his own mother. She was a very good homemaker. She had taught her four sons to be good at taking care of a house, always saying that one day they may be living on their own and would need to be able to help themselves.

He and his older brother, the one before him, gravitated toward their father's traits, as from an early age he took them everywhere with him.

His father was a handyman, a jack-of-all-trades. His eldest brother shifted toward the operation and repair of engines and electronic items. His younger brother was more into academics, desiring to become a teacher, and he (Joshua) loved fixing things. He eventually attended a technical college and learned carpentry, which he loved.

Joshua's love for fixing things made him such an asset to his household. If there was furniture to be rearranged or rugs to be placed or replaced, you would hear, "Call Joshua." In response he would always come with a willing attitude, and when the task was complete, you would always hear someone say, "Wow! Boy, you're good. You made that look so easy."

Whatever Joshua did, he did as if it was for a member of the royal family. He always gave it his best.

Joshua tried hard not to act upon his feelings for Tianna. He would go to her house to pay his rent, but even at those instances he would not say much. He always had so much to say, so many questions to ask, but he never did. It just never felt like the right time, but he was confident that the right time would come.

This right time would come, however, in a way he never imagined.

CHAPTER 4

It was such a bright and beautiful sunny morning. At least that's how it started out.

The news was spreading fast. Hurricane Irma, with category 4 force winds, was gaining strength and heading for the British Virgin Islands. The disaster management director was on the morning news report encouraging residents to board up their homes, as the hurricane was expected to make landfall by midweek.

Tianna was home for the day, as she worked from her home office on Mondays. Having a home office was something she wanted when she lived in the little wooden house. Seeing that there was not enough space for a table and cabinet, she was inspired to move into the main house when the last tenant moved out.

The main house offered two spacious bedrooms and a bathroom with a tub, one that she had purchased specifically for the purpose of having evening bubble baths. There was a cozy living room, an eat-in kitchen, with a porch at the front and the back of the house. There was enough space for her to "spread out." This was a term she used for having a lot of space, uncluttered and free, especially for her "dance moments," which took up a whole room—or two. She always thought to herself that she could never dance on a dance floor as she did at home, or she would knock down a few folks. This would always make her smile to herself.

She made a few calls based on her things-to-do list, updated some reports, and took a break for lunch.

After the break, Tianna's eyes caught an outfit she had been working on. The outfit consisted of a skirt and a matching case for her Bible, both of which she then completed. She figured that she would complete the top after the hurricane had passed, and that it would be her "Hurricane Irma swag."

When she was finished sewing, she decided to put her sewing machines and other electronic items in the living room. This was followed by some other items that she had put off putting away. Although she felt quite safe, somehow at this point she also felt compelled to move some items out of her bedroom.

It was after five o'clock when she heard a knock at the door. She peeped out the window and did not see a vehicle. She was grabbing her robe when she heard the knock again.

"Hello?" she called out.

"Yes, it's me," the voice responded.

Joshua was at the door. She could recognize his voice anywhere.

"I'm coming," she shouted as she grabbed the receipt book and a pen and slipped them into a pocket of her robe.

"Hi," she said when she got to the door.

"Yeah, hi, Ms. Te," he answered, and handed her the crisp hundred dollar bills.

She counted them with a little nervousness and wrote the date on the receipt.

"I heard there's a storm coming—category 5," Joshua shared, softening the thick silence that was between them for a few minutes.

"Category 5 now?" she questioned in a surprised tone of voice as she looked into his eyes.

"Yeah," he responded.

Their eyes stayed focused on each other for a few seconds. She then looked back at the receipt book and fought to take the page out as if she was doing it for the first time. Being in Joshua's presence always seemed to make her feel so incapacitated. Things that she would do with ease became mammoth tasks when he was around.

"I hope it goes in another direction and we only get some rain," she said.

"I don't even think we can take much rain now, after the flood last month," Joshua exclaimed.

"I know."

Again there was a silence as they both reflected on the flooding almost a month before.

It was August Monday, the most anticipated day of the annual emancipation celebrations. Scores of people would travel from all around the world just to be a part of the celebrations on this day.

The previous events had gone well. Gospel fest, which marked the official opening of the festival village and featured a number of guest artists including international recording artist, Myron Butler, was well supported; the Calypso King was crowned; the new Miss British Virgin Islands had already secured her spot in the hall of fame of BVI Queens; the 2017 Prince and Princess were crowned; other pre-events had already taken place, and the Neil "Mr. Melee" Blyden Festiville was declared open.

On that unforgettable Monday, troupes, which are made up of individuals dressed in festive wear doing performances; floats, which are decorated platforms mounted on a truck carrying a display in the parade procession depicting the theme; and floupes, which are a combination of both a troupe and a float, paraded the streets in bright beautiful colors to music just for that occasion— calypso, soca, and fungi. There were also individual entries with some highlighting the traditional ways of life. These included a showcase of items that were used by the generations before, such as the ironing goose. The ironing goose was used to iron clothes. It was a heavy metal iron that was operated with hot coals. There was the yard broom that was made of certain dry sticks, and many other items.

The parade culminated at the festival village, where booths were lined up in all colors of the rainbow, and the colorful flags swayed in the wind, as if dancing to the music.

Upon arrival at the village, there was a plethora of food and drinks. On this particular day, many persons would be prepared to devour a plate of their favorite food: pig tail, salt fish and green banana, peas and rice with stewed oxtail, and many more. Of course, the national dish of fungi and boiled fish was a must-have. These would be washed down with local juices like passion fruit, sorrel, and lime.

There was live entertainment and rides for the children. It was expected to be a *grand full-moon affair*.

However, only Mother Nature enjoyed the wet fete that afternoon. Some rain was forecasted, but no one anticipated such an unparalleled occurrence of seventeen inches of rain within a few hours. When residents and visitors emerged from their places of hibernation after the rainfall, they marveled to see the extent of the damage. As a matter of fact, several homes were flooded so much so that those individuals lost everything. Alternative housing had to be arranged for them.

The thought that persons were already displaced, coupled with the horrific stories they had heard of hurricane-ravaged countries led them both to a moment of reflection.

"Well, I hope we'll be okay," Joshua's voice jolted Tianna back to reality as she felt so sorry for those persons who had to be uprooted from the comfort of their homes to temporary housing.

"Me too. I'm sure we will," she said as Joshua turned to leave.

"Have a good evening."

"You too. And if it gets too stormy up there, you can always come by me."

"Thanks, Ms. Te, I will be fine."

"All right," Tianna said as she shrugged her shoulders.

When Tianna got back to her room, she took the money and other contents from her pocket and threw them on her bed.

"Geez," she said to herself. "What were you thinking inviting Joshua to come here? The man has a brother living up the hill. What makes you think he would want to come by you? Besides, just because you are attracted to him doesn't mean he's attracted to you."

She smiled to herself.

"Well, that twinkle in his eyes whenever he looks at me says a lot."

She put her hand to her heart.

"Okay, Tia," she said with as much drama as a military commander to his crew. "Stop the negative self-talk. What was said, was said. It cannot be taken back. If Joshua needs to come here, he will. If not, oh well!"

For many years, Tianna struggled with entertaining negative self-talk. She would try to surround herself with positive people and memorize Bible verses and quotes that encouraged her to think positive, but it was a long battle.

It was not until she started seeing a counselor that she realized that the power to change her mindset truly rested within her. Armed with that new insight, she focused more on seeing the best in others, listening and reading self-help material, and ensuring that she did not accept energies into her spirit that were not positive.

Tianna went to her desk, prepared a deposit slip for the money Joshua paid her, and wrote a list of things to do. She intended to go into town the following day.

A few minutes later, she looked out of the window and it looked cloudy. She then looked at the time on her iPod.

"Oh my, I will be late for prayer meeting," she said as she scrambled to find her cell phone. "Let me call someone to come and give me a ride."

When she arrived at the church, the prayer meeting had not started. She checked the time and realized that it was five minutes past starting time. Nevertheless, the person in charge walked in just behind her and proceeded to their assignment.

Tianna always loved attending church, even in her teen years. Whenever her peers would talk about not wanting to go to church after they turned eighteen, she could not relate. As an adult and after all that she had been through in her life, praying meant a lot to her. To her, no other relationship was more valuable than staying in close communion with her God.

The church she attended was among the biggest on the island. It was designed and built by her bishop, who was a contractor. There were three levels: the basement, which was underground, the fellowship hall, which was on the first floor, and the main sanctuary.

Although having a basement was an unusual building feature in the BVI, when the cistern was built, an area was included for worship while the building was being completed.

The fellowship hall area housed the kitchen, offices, and bathrooms. Special events like prayer breakfast, after-church lunches, and special dinners were held in this area.

There were two sets of stairs from the front and back of the building to the main sanctuary. A wheelchair ramp led right from the road to the front door of the church.

On the inside padded blue pews lined four rows, from right to left, and the floor was carpeted wall to wall with a matching blue carpet. Royal blue drapes adorned the pulpit area, just behind the choir loft.

On the pulpit, there was an area for the drummer, the guitar player, and the person playing the keyboard. The brown hardwood podium stood in the center in such a way that as one entered the building, they would have a direct view of whoever was at the podium.

On this night, the prayer meeting was being held in the basement. The attendance size was significantly lower at a prayer meeting service, and thus it made for a cozy gathering.

Before closing off, the small group gathered in a circle, and prayer requests were made. One person took charge and assigned individuals to pray for the different requests.

Tianna was asked to pray for a sister and niece who were traveling to St. Vincent that same night. The concern was that the storm was approaching and their safety could be compromised. Although she preferred to pray in private, Tianna nevertheless embraced the opportunity to approach the throne of grace on their behalf.

After church, as was customary, members gathered in groups for an after-church fellowship. Tianna was not one to attach herself to any particular group. Thus, she just went around greeting everyone. As she stood waiting for a ride home, she observed that Hurricane Irma was the topic of choice in many of the groups.

Persons shared their experiences with hurricanes, as well as stories they heard from their grandparents and other persons, along with documentaries seen on television.

It appeared that almost everyone felt or hoped that *Irma* would take a detour as many other hurricanes had done over the past several years.

C H A P T E R

Tuesday morning arrived with overcast skies.

Tianna prayed and read Proverbs 5. She had made it a habit to read a proverb each day as a means of ensuring that she stayed in the Word. This was followed by a prayer for guidance and protection for that day.

When she was finished, she tuned in to ZBVI Radio Station, something she did every morning at six o'clock for as long as she could remember.

Each month she would send out birthday and anniversary greetings on the station to celebrants she knew. Some folks got so accustomed to the greetings that every now and then someone would say, "You forgot me?" or "Someone told me they heard the greeting and I knew it could only be you."

Apart from the devotions, ZBVI Radio was always up to date with the latest in local news. With a hurricane on the way, it was the radio station of choice—not just for Tianna but for the majority of the territory. It was a great source of comfort through previous major hurricanes like Hurricane Hugo in 1989 and Marilyn in 1995.

This morning, she particularly wanted to get an update on Hurricane Irma. It seemed like it was on a mission to visit the islands, with no sign of changing course. The disaster management director was admonishing residents to rush their final preparations for hurricane readiness. In her report, she pointed out that boarding up windows and doors should be completed by midday. Vehicle owners were told to fill their vehicles with gas, and everyone was encouraged to purchase food for several days, especially nonperishable goods, and ensure that their essential documents were secured in ziplock bags if possible and placed in a safe place, or taken with them to the hurricane shelter if they needed to move. She also encouraged persons to take all medications with them.

By the time the news report ended, Tianna was ready to leave the house. She was getting an early start as her vehicle had been in the shop for a few months. She hoped to get a quick ride to get in and out of town as fast as possible.

Her first stop in town was the bank. When she arrived, there was a long line of people waiting for it to open. She secured a spot, put her earphones in her ears, and pulled out her papers. She decided to do some work on a book she was writing.

Tianna always loved to write. From the time she knew herself, she was always at peace and quite comfortable with a pen or pencil and a book or piece of paper.

While in primary school, she would take clean pages from her schoolbooks and make birthday cards for her friends, complete with poems that she composed. She would decorate the front of the card as creatively as she could and, in her best handwriting, include her poem.

As she got older, she was introduced to modern devices that allowed her to make notes and store them. However, regardless of what device she was introduced to, she maintained a habit of also writing down the information. She felt that she was more likely to recall the information with it written in her handwriting.

Tianna also loved office work and was good at it. This gave her a desire to start her own business. Her only challenge was that she had so many business ideas. She would get hyped planning a particular business venture, do as much research as she could, take a course, and get cold feet when the process moved her out of her comfort zone. She would take one step forward, entertain a few criticisms and negative self-talks, and retreat.

Nevertheless, the opportunity had finally come, just three years before, when the manager at the radio station where she worked sent her an email, asking her to turn in her keys at the end of the day, as the result of some negotiations. She was taken aback.

Tianna had submitted a proposal to change the nature of her employment to commission based. She had been hired to be the sales representative. Although she did just about everything, such as voicing ads and doing the groundwork for new programs, her primary duty was sales. Management had agreed to 25 percent commission in the initial meeting. When it was time to finalize the contract, the commission amount was changed to 15 percent. Tianna could not agree to the new amount. Thus, the situation ended in a heartbreak for her.

For the next two weeks, she stayed at home and nursed her wounded spirit.

She tried to find some comfort in reading her Bible and could not understand at the time why she was led to Ezekiel 37—the valley of dry bones. She certainly felt like she was in a valley of dry bones and that there was no way out. Even with bills to pay, she did not want to get out of bed.

A leader in her church met her in town on the first day after her dismissal and relayed their version of the story. On the basis that she had some respect for that leader according to their position, she shared how disappointed she felt at what happened. The conversations on her situation continued, but only made her feel more hopeless. That individual seemed to be using her situation to fuel their own personal disgruntled state.

She even started hearing rumors that she had already made alternate plans. This made her want to just cut off everyone.

It was not until she started to change her focus that things started to fall into place.

One day, while at home, she picked up the book *No Matter What* by Lisa Nichols. Her sister Dee had given her a copy of the book after attending Lisa's presentation at the H. Lavity Stoutt Community College. Although Tianna had previously taken up the book to read, she never got past page 3. Yet she found that she could not put the book down at this crossroad in her life—five years later.

It was the section about "From Anger to Action" that would make the greatest impact on adjusting her mind-set. To answer the questions "What do you want?" and "What would make you happy?" Tianna concluded that she no longer wanted to work a nine-to-five job on someone else's terms. She wanted to be in a position to get up on a Monday morning and decide to get a full-body massage; she wanted to write books and travel the world, telling her stories of overcoming many obstacles. She wanted to have the time and financial resources to volunteer with humanitarian organizations, to be able to help those in need. She wanted to ultimately make a difference in other people's lives.

Today, however, she was working on one of the many books that she started. She made up in her mind that she would complete this one, as she saw it as her ticket to *"living the life she wanted,"* according to Lisa Nichols.

When she had completed her transaction at that bank, she went to another bank. She was next in line when the weatherman on the overhead television screen caught her attention. He was forecasting Hurricane Irma, and he shared that he had visited the British Virgin Islands two years before.

"The islands," he said, "are an archipelago of islands in the Caribbean with four main islands and several smaller ones—Tortola being the largest. It is known as the sailing capital of the world and has white sandy beaches with clear pristinely blue waters. On Virgin Gorda is the Baths, a maze of boulders on the beach that will entice swimmers and adventurers alike. Jost Van Dyke boasts the famous Foxy's Beach Bar, and Anegada, which is flat, offers a memorable diving experience of the Wreck of the Rhone, just off its shores."

"According to what I'm seeing in the weather forecast with Hurricane Irma approaching, it does not look good for Road Town, the capital of Tortola. I don't want to say it," he paused, "but I have to say it."

Just then, a tap on the shoulder by the person behind her jolted Tianna from her focus. That was followed immediately by a chorus of "next," from everyone behind her, it seemed. She hurried to the teller and was out of there in no time.

Town was busy. Supermarket lines were cart to cart with people doing their last-minute shopping; gas stations were backed up with vehicles to be filled up; and traffic lines were bumper to bumper, with lumber protruding from just about every other vehicle.

When it was time to leave town, Tianna stood in the area of the Port Purcell roundabout to get a ride. She had decided to do her last-minute grocery shopping in East End, closer to home. A kind lady stopped to give her a ride. When she got into the vehicle, she recognized that it was the sister of her late godfather, who was laid to rest a few weeks before. As they journeyed on, they talked about the hustle and bustle and preparations being made.

In all her conversations, Tianna shared that she had fond memories of hurricanes past. Her family, she recalled, would all be gathered together in one house, with the food of choice in abundance—a tin of crackers. Hurricane Hugo was particularly memorable for her, not because of the available crackers but because as the hurricane grew worse, her dad gathered his wife and six children and led them to safety at a neighbor's house, holding hands as they journeyed.

When the family returned home, the wooden house was still standing. However, the sea, which was very close to the house, had come up and flooded the house; dishes floated out of the cupboards, and her mom's nice carpet was no longer looking or smelling nice. They all banded together, cleaned up the place, and slowly got back to normal.

Tianna made a few stops when she got to East End. Before heading home, though, she bought a warm loaf of bread from Honey & Spice Bakery and a few other food items from the supermarket in the area.

She got a ride, this time with her god-brother, the son of the same godfather that had passed away recently. He lived in another area, but for her safety he took her home. When he noticed that the windows of her house were not boarded up, there was great concern on his face. He did question her about it, but Tianna gave him a convenient answer, as it was almost five o'clock and no one was expected to be out and about. There was nothing that could be done about it at that point.

CHAPTER 6

The wind was blowing strong on the outside, but it was a beautiful Wednesday morning, one that Tianna, and certainly the entire population of the British Virgin Islands, would not soon forget. It was the day that would change their lives forever.

Tianna prayed and read Proverbs 6 before fixing some breakfast. This was her kind of day. The electricity was off. The usual distractions were nonexistent. Today, she could actually focus on getting something to eat. Eating breakfast was a real struggle in the morning. Her mind was usually consumed with all kind of things she needed to do. On a normal day, breakfast was just a conversational piece in her mind.

With the windows on one side of her bedroom open, she enjoyed the cool breeze. The other windows served as her television screen to all the activities happening on the outside.

There was a wooden structure under construction that had recently started. It appeared to be an extension to the poultry farm that was located on the hill across from her house. It was in her direct view. It was the first structure she noticed being dismantled.

She then noticed a wooden house in close proximity to the farm. There was something on it that was flapping in the wind. She wanted to get a better view, so she pulled out her binoculars.

At one point, she acted on the premonition that she needed to put things like her sewing machines and laptop in a more secure area, outside of her bedroom.

When she returned to the window with her binoculars, she saw what looked like curtains flapping in the wind, over the roof of the wooden house.

"Oh dear! I hope no one is in there," she muttered to herself.

She took a break and decided to continue with her pack up efforts. As she entered the living room to put some items there, a hard wind blew. This drew her attention toward the kitchen window.

"Praise be unto your name, Lord God," she prayed with a loud voice, as if God was deaf. "You are God of the storm and God in the storm. Lord, you said, 'Peace, be still,' and the winds and the waves obeyed your command. Grant your servant that same sweet peace in the midst of this storm I pray.

The wind subsided a bit.

Suddenly there was a thunderous knock at the door. Tianna jumped. She spun around, grabbed her chest, and leaned over, breathing deeply.

"Peace, Lord, peace," she said, trying to catch her breath.

"Ms. Te, Ms. Te," the voice echoed in panic.

Her heart started beating so hard that it sounded like a band was playing in her chest.

"Joshua?" she whispered.

"Ms. Te!"

"I'm coming, I'm coming," Tianna she said as she hurried to the bedroom to get her keys, as the door could only be opened with the keys.

When she opened the door, Joshua hurried in. She slammed the door shut, and for what seemed like a very long time to Joshua, she fumbled to lock it.

"Do you want me to help you?" Joshua asked.

"No, it's okay. I got it."

When she finally got the door locked, with her back turned to him, she took a deep breath. Every joint in her body always felt so weak when he was around. She tried to appear strong and well composed at all times. At this particular time, she was not sure she was doing a good job at it, but she was trying real hard.

"You nearly scared the gajebas out of me. What happened?" she asked, taking another deep breath.

"The house started shaking. I was wondering whether I should get out or not, as I could see galvanize, tree limbs, and all kind of things flying by. That last hard wind took the bathroom section, so I took a run for it when it got a little calm. I was going to my brother's house, but concluded that here was closer."

"Your elbow is bleeding."

"It's just a bruise. I slipped coming down the hill. I almost hung myself on the electrical wire across your driveway."

"Well, I'm glad you're safe," she said as she cleaned up his wound with the items she retrieved while he was speaking.

Although she did not think she would need it, Tianna had gotten a first aid kit. Thus, it felt good to have one on hand.

She was never very comfortable at the sight of blood, but had gained some confidence when she took a first aid course being offered by the Red Cross when she was a volunteer leader of the Girl Guide Association. Joshua just allowed her to do her thing. For him there was no need to make a fuss, it was only a bruise.

Tianna and Joshua did not even notice the wind had gotten stronger until there was a big crashing sound. Since Tianna was finished attending to Joshua's bruise, she put away the first aid kit and hurried to the window. When she looked out, she saw a piece of galvanize with pieces of two by four attached to it.

"Gosh, do you think that's part of the house roof?" she asked Joshua as if she expected him to be intimately knowledgeable of his house roof that he would recognize it flying around.

"It could be. I wouldn't doubt it with the way that wind sounds."

The wind orchestra on the outside was very powerful. Tianna was becoming more and more concerned. It sounded as though the back of the house was being used in the musical ensemble.

At one point, as they both stood in the living room listening, there was a loud bang on the house. Tianna jumped next to Joshua. He held her gently until she seemed to catch her breath.

"Are you scared?" he asked.

"I'm trying not to be. I know God is in the midst of it all. I just don't like hearing those sounds out there."

Moments later, everything was still.

"Do you hear that?" Joshua asked.

"Hear what?"

"Exactly! It is calm. The wind is not even blowing."

Tianna led the way to the kitchen, opened the backdoor, and went out. When she looked for the house, it was not there.

"Oh, Joshua, the house is completely gone. What will you do?"

"What do you want to do?"

"I don't know. What do you think?"

"I say rebuild."

"Then rebuild it is."

After a brief chat with a few neighbors who had ventured outside in the calm of the storm, Tianna declared that she was going back inside as the wind had started picking up again.

Tianna went in ahead of Joshua. It took him a few minutes and a strong yank on the door to get it closed. He then joined Tianna as she stood in the kitchen.

A hard wind blew, and Tianna shouted and repeated, "Praise be unto your name Lord God."

Sparing no time, the wind blew harder and harder. Then they heard a loud sound of glass breaking.

"The bedroom," Tianna said in a panic. She pushed past Joshua and headed for her bedroom. She immediately grabbed the doorknob and slammed the door shut. But before she could get any satisfaction from what she thought was a brilliant idea, the wind pulled the door open, dragging her with it and slamming it shut on her left hand, hitting her on her left cheekbone, knocking her to the ground.

Joshua had followed her when she headed for the bedroom, but before he could say or do anything, she was on the ground.

He had barely helped her to her feet when the front door flew open, and she pushed him aside again and dashed to close it.

"Ms. Te, no!" Joshua shouted as he rushed to her, grabbed her around her waist, and closed the door shut with his foot. He dragged a couch and affixed it behind the door after he was certain that she was back on her feet.

Breathlessly Tianna watched as Joshua secured the door with that heavy couch her mother had given her just over a year before.

"Let's go to the bathroom," she suggested.

She led the way, and together they went to safety.

CHAPTER 7

Tianna and Joshua were now in the safety of her bathroom. The bathroom was Tianna's favorite room in the house. She always liked a nice small bathroom and had plans to one day repaint it blue—different shades of blue. The color was inspired by her childhood bathroom. In her mind all bathrooms should be blue.

Joshua pulled Tianna close to him and held her gently as they stood in the bathroom listening to the wind outside. In an attempt to relax, she took a deep breath and rested her head on his chest.

"I'm here for you, Ms. Te. Let me protect you," he whispered in her ear.

With no response from her, he raised her up and cupped her face in his hands. He then realized that the left side of her face was swollen.

"Your face is swollen. Did you hurt your eye?"

"No."

"Why is it different to the other one?" He paused. "If you don't mind me asking?"

"You can ask whatever you want. I don't have to answer," she said with a smiling face.

"I'm sorry."

"Sorry, for what?" she asked, with big invisible question marks all over her forehead. "It's okay. I was in a car accident that injured my eye and left me with a detached retina, damaged lens and cornea. The cells in the cornea are dying and losing their transparency. That is why the eye looks the way it does. Well, according to the doctor." She smiled.

"I would really like to hear what happened," Joshua said, with great concern in his voice.

"Sure, as long as we are alive after all the excitement going on outside there."

"I feel certain that we will be."

"If it is the Lord's will."

"In the meantime, do you have anything I can put on it to massage it a little?"

"I have some honey."

"Honey?" he questioned as she reached in the bathroom cabinet.

"In the bathroom," he again questioned, with great curiosity.

"Yessiree! Honey in the bathroom," she answered.

"What is this supposed to do?"

"It is supposed to create a moistened condition around the wound with its antibacterial activity, which would provide a barrier that prevents infection. Besides, I prefer natural remedies."

"Yes, ma'am. You sure have a strong conviction about honey!"

"Yup, I do."

Joshua put some honey in his hand and gently massaged her swollen left cheek.

"You must have seen stars when that door hit you in the face," he said.

"I got a glimpse of gloryland." She chuckled.

He smiled.

"Are you a Christian?" he asked.

"Yep! Are you?"

"I was."

"What happened?"

"Long story."

Although that response left her with many questions, Tianna did not think it was the time or place to ask any further questions on the matter.

"By the way," he said with a look of great concern on his face, "how is your hand?"

She lifted her left hand in his view.

"A bit swollen," she declared.

"That does not look just a bit swollen to me. Is it hurting?"

"No. It's not hurting at all."

"No?" he questioned. He found it hard to believe after seeing how hard the bedroom door closed in on her hand. He had gotten to where she was just in time to see the door closing in. It just seemed to have happened in a matter of seconds.

"Your hand must be made of steel," he joked. "How does your face feel now?"

"A lot better since you worked your magic on it. It only hurts when I move it around."

She made funny faces, and they both laughed.

The bathroom door jolted them out of their laughter as it swung open wide and slammed shut. Tianna hurriedly but carefully stepped into the tub and shouted for Joshua to put the two buckets of water she had collected behind the door.

As soon as he did, the door swung open again, pushing the two buckets of water toward the tub and splashing water in their faces like the swells on Josiah's Bay Beach.

Joshua grabbed the shower curtain rod, which was on the floor. Tianna had taken off the curtain earlier in the day when the wind was blowing strongly through the window, as she was unable to close the window.

As soon as he caught himself and wiped the water from his face, Joshua positioned one of the rectangular buckets beside the tub and put the rod between the door and the bucket to prevent the door from opening.

He then looked at Tianna, whose wrap was well soaked with water. Since he did not get as wet as she did, he took his shirts off and gave her his undershirt. Before she could say anything, he turned his back to her and allowed her to remove the wet wrap and change into something drier.

A new day had dawned, and while it was still windy on the outside, it was nothing like the winds that had blown in his landlady's window, or should he say former landlady. After all, she could no longer be his landlady if there was no longer a house to rent.

"We will rebuild," he whispered to himself, being careful not to awaken Tianna.

The petite body of the woman of his dreams lay resting peacefully beside him. He could not believe that he had slept so comfortably in a bathtub with someone else. A twin- or full-sized bed was too small for him, and even from his teen days he never liked a small bed. Yet here he was.

"Oh, the things that hurricanes can make you do." He quietly chuckled to himself.

Joshua eased his way out of the tub, trying his best not to disturb Tianna. When he stepped out, he almost fell, as the floor was covered with water. The two bath mats were soaked. He removed the shower curtain rod and pulled the doorknob, to no avail. He observed the lock for a few minutes and realized that he needed a *MacGyver trick*. He looked around and found a plastic fork, which he pushed between the door and the frame as he turned the knob. When the door opened, he found that there was more water, along with glass, clothes, paper, leaves, and dirt everywhere, including on the walls. It was the first time he had been in Tianna's house.

When he looked to his left, the horrific scene of Tianna being tossed to and fro by the bedroom door haunted him. He felt so terrible that he could not prevent her from getting hurt, as everything happened so fast. Nevertheless, he was glad that she did not lose consciousness. The door she tried to save was now rolled up like cardboard and lying in water, completely dismantled. It looked like everything that could blow away had left Tianna's room and was in the hallway and on the living-room floor.

On his right was a closed door. He wondered what was behind it and why Ms. Te didn't go in there instead. Was she hiding something or someone? *Maybe I'll find out someday*, he thought to himself.

He then walked as cautiously as he could through the water and the debris to the kitchen. One of the windows was broken. It blew inside. He picked it up and looked at it. It did not look as though it would need to be replaced, but that would have to be checked out another time. Some of the cupboards had blown open and the food items were all over the kitchen floor. It was a big mess!

His attention was then turned to the front door, which was still in place, secured by the couch he had put there, but the glass had fallen out. He picked up the glass, and as he examined it, he realized that it was not even scratched.

"Wow," he said to himself, "this is good material."

Tianna opened her eyes and saw light coming through the bathroom window.

"Thank you, Lord, for this beautiful day that you have made. I will rejoice and be glad in it," she prayed.

She then noticed that the door was open and that Joshua was not there. She carefully stepped into the water, glanced at her hurricane-ravaged bedroom, and saw Joshua sweeping out water through the space under the back door.

"Morning, Ms. Te."

"Morning! Have you been up long?"

"Just a few minutes. Did you know that some people put a drain in their kitchen and bathroom floors when they build, so that in cases like this, they don't have to sweep out water? The water just drains off."

"Wow! That would be a nice feature to have right now."

"Well, now that you have the idea, you can incorporate it when you build again."

"True. Thank you. I will certainly keep that in mind. Did you look out?" she asked, peeping out the broken kitchen window.

"Yes, a bit. From what I can see, many of the neighbors got a beating from Irma."

"Have you checked on your brother?"

"Not yet. I wanted to make sure you were okay first."

"Well, you should go do that now. Let him know that you're okay and see how he's doing."

"Are you sure you'll be okay?" He held her face to his. "Your eye looks like someone beat you up."

"Irma did, remember."

"I don't want to remember that scene. I hate to think of the fact that there was nothing I could do. It happened so fast."

"Just being here was a big help."

"There is a pole across the road that I can see from here. I don't even want to imagine what the road leading up here is like. Every little rain washes it away. Anyway, you may not be able to go to the hospital today."

"I'm still not in any pain, so don't worry about it. Just go see about your brother."

They both walked toward the front door.

"Oh boy, the glass came out," she said. "I'm glad it did not come out when we were out here. It might have hit one of us."

"You are one amazing lady. What were you thinking holding back those doors?"

"I don't know. I guess I wasn't thinking."

"Nanna always told us to stay away from windows, doors, and telephones whenever there is a hurricane."

"Who is Nanna?"

"My grandmother."

"Did she experience a hurricane like Irma?"

"No, but she told her grandchildren the stories her parents told her. She said when she was a child there was a hurricane, and although their wooden house was not destroyed, the roof was making a lot of noise in the wind."

"I guess persons like you and me will have to be the Nannas of today, passing on the lessons learned from Hurricane Irma."

"Yep. That's true. They cannot know if we don't tell them. Anyway, I will get some tools and return to fix the front and back doors after checking in with my brother."

"What's wrong with the back door?"

"It's jammed shut."

After Joshua left, Tianna decided to look for her cell phone to see the time. She did not find it on the entertainment center where she thought she left it, but found her iPod instead. This, she thought, was strange, because they were supposed to be together.

Although she had no idea of the state of the island as a whole, she felt isolated in her corner without her phone. She thought of her mom, dad, and siblings and just hoped that they were all right.

CHAPTER 8

Tianna lived in an area where the nearest visible house to hers was under construction. The others were a five-minute walk away. Although she did not intend to leave her home for the day with so much cleaning to do, the rest of her family members were on her mind. Thinking that they often said that she lived far away, she figured she would have to be the one to touch base with them. With this in mind, she got busy sweeping out water and picking up all the paper and clothes that littered her house.

"Inside," a voice called from the outside. It was her sister, Dee.

Dee was very unique in the family, as she was the shortest of the siblings, taking on their father's stature. Tianna was favored with siblings that she loved. Three sisters and two brothers followed her. Even though there was one sister between them, Tianna and Dee had bonded very well at an early age. They had a lot in common. They both could design and construct their own garments. They both had an interest in business ownership and were once headliners in a local newspaper as rivals for a top spot in the H. Lavity Stoutt Community College's two-mile college classic race series. While it was just good fun and exercise for Tianna, it was a dream come true for Dee, who always loved track and field and had a desire to participate but was too timid to pursue it in high school.

Nevertheless, as she participated in the two-mile college classic series, one of the local sports enthusiasts saw her raw talent and decided to coach her. She went on to break the women's college classic series record, then demolished her own record. As a matter of fact, one year, a young athlete was said to have trained just to take her top spot in the series.

Dee had opportunities to travel and compete regionally and went on to set a new national record in the three-thousand-meter race.

Although by this time she had held off on racing, she was clad as an Olympic champion. The black-and-pink suit hugged her body, which had filled out nicely since she stopped running consistently. The sneakers and socks were the perfect match.

"Morning, Dee, how are you," Tianna greeted her sister with a hug.

"I'm good. Happy to be alive."

"How did you get here?"

"Girl, Tia, you don't want to see the place. It's a total devastation. I just walked from Brandywine Bay, and it is unbelievable," she said as she removed her sneakers and carefully walked around on the floor that was still covered with water and debris.

"We have so much to give thanks for," Tianna responded.

"Girl, I saw some people going through the rubble of what was once their home, trying to see what they could find to salvage."

Dee whipped her camera out of the handbag she was carrying and started scrolling through to show Tianna the extent of the damages she had captured.

"First of all," she continued with her reporting, "most of the road is impassable to the motoring public because of large trees, poles, parts of house roofs—it is a mess. A pole fell on someone's apartment and was partially in the window. Yachts that were anchored in their area of safety are now bundled together, some on the shoreline as if they were each trying to get away from the rough water, and others sank.

"The wayside bar just before the corner to go to the college blew away, and a catamaran had become the new shelter for the bar. As for water, the gut in Paraquita Bay is still running, flooding the road."

After they had gone through the pictures, Dee explained what was happening in each video.

"As I was walking along, more and more people were emerging from their homes and were on the street," Dee continued. "I saw one guy looking up at his home that had no roof. When I asked him what he did during the storm, he said that he, his wife, and four year-old son were running from room to room as the roof lifted in each section of the house where they were."

In one of the video clips she shared, there were many persons out and about looking at the damages. In another, one section of a store was just rubble. The other section, which was a trailer, was perfectly fine until a pounding sound could be heard in the video, which she shared was someone pounding the trailer until it opened. When that feat was accomplished, persons could be seen taking away all kinds of household goods—new ironing boards and other items.

Just across the street from all that activity was a trailer that was upside down, resting on the front end of a vehicle that was also upside down.

"This recovery will take about six months to a year," was Dee's estimated recovery time based on the extent of the damages she saw, just in the East End area.

"So how are things at the house?" Tianna finally asked about the family house in which Dee lived.

"Girl, Tia, thank God nothing happened to the windows or the sliding door. The wind was so strong that I was praying that the window didn't burst open. I was so scared it would just blow open. I have never heard anything like that."

"Well, I hurt my hand," Tianna informed her.

"How?"

"I was trying to close the bedroom door after the window blew out. The wind opened the door with its full force, sucking me with it and closing it on my hand."

"I'm glad it's not worse."

"Yeah, me too."

Tianna did not mention Joshua's presence, as she did not feel it was the right time.

"I'll start making my way home," Dee said as she was putting her sneakers on.

They both went outside and viewed the damages done to the neighboring houses.

"Did you see my top house?" Tianna asked Dee.

"No, what happened to it?"

"It's completely gone."

"I hope the tenant was not in it," Dee exclaimed with deep concern. "Do you know if he is okay?"

"Yes, he's fine."

Dee looked Tianna full in her face with a confused look, as she asked about the tenant's safety.

"Wait a minute, did you hurt your face too?"

"Yes, but it already feels like it is healing."

"Oh, okay. I'll head back now. Heavy-equipment operators have already started clearing the road, so I hope it's better on my way back. I just don't want to get hurt," Dee said.

"How are Mom and Dad?" Tianna asked before Dee left.

"Mom and Dad are okay. They had no damage, just water. But, girl, I was really scared that the window in my kitchen would blow out. I am so glad it didn't."

"Have you heard from Jan?" Tianna questioned.

Jan was the sister between Tianna and Dee. She had gone on vacation with her best friend the week before the hurricane and was scheduled to return the Tuesday before the hurricane was expected. The last news Tianna heard about them was that they had made it to St. Thomas. However, since the ports of entry closed at noon that same day, Jan and her friend had to ride out the storm in St. Thomas.

"No, but I hope she's okay."

"Yeah, me too. Anyway, you be safe, and thanks for stopping by."

After Dee left, Tianna paused for a few minutes to observe the neighboring houses. She could see that those that still had roofs, had multiple windows damaged. One neighbor had three tall coconut trees in his front yard. Irma obviously took those when she was leaving, as they were now nowhere in sight. Another neighbor had completely lost the section of the roof that she could see, and there were two vehicles hanging over a bank and resting on the back of the house.

As Tianna continued looking, she realized that the number of houses she could see from her location had increased significantly. She saw houses she did not even know existed. All the trees were just sticks, and all the nearby locations were visible. She even got to see things she had always wondered about, like where a particular neighbor had their pool, based on the section of the house that could only be seen from the road. Everything was exposed.

CHAPTER 9

Moments after Tianna found her cell phone in a pool of water on her bedroom floor, a vehicle drove into the yard. Her face was filled with invisible question marks.

"Who could that be," she whispered.

Before she could push the pile of wet debris out of the way and exit her door-less bedroom, her mom shouted, "Hello" from the opening in the front of the house where there was a door just the day before.

"Mom," she said with the excitement of a child who was waiting to be picked up from school after a hard day.

Tianna was so happy to see her mom. Although her mom had celebrated her seventy-fifth birthday just a few weeks before, she could pass as Tianna's big sister. She was tall—a lot taller than her husband. Her face was smooth and wrinkle-free. Her hair was well groomed, and her clothes were always well shaped since she could make and alter them herself.

The older lady opened her arms and gave her eldest child a hug. "How are you?" she asked as she squeezed Tianna in her embrace.

"Me? I'm wonderful," Tianna responded. "I'm alive, and where there is life there is hope."

"Hello," her dad's voice sounded in the background.

"My sweet daddy!" she exclaimed as she rushed over to give him a peck on the cheek.

Her dad was five years older than her mom. He was a hard worker, and it showed. Tianna liked the way each wrinkle seemed to somehow create character to his features. If she had her way, she would take black-and-white pictures of his face every time she saw him—in all directions, with different expressions.

Apart from the fact that he had been troubled with some neck pains and was moving a bit sluggishly, he was in fairly good health and looked just as happy to see her.

"You took a beating up here," he exclaimed.

"You see that, huh."

"Well, thank God for life. It could have been worse," her dad said to provide some encouragement.

"That's so true," she replied.

"Whaz up," a subtle bass voice said.

Tianna looked around to see her brother Lee standing not too far behind her dad. She was so consumed with her dad that she had not even notice him.

"I'm good. You look dry," she quipped.

"What's that supposed to mean?" he said, disconcerted.

"You look like the storm didn't blow your way."

He threw back his head and laughed out loud.

"You don't want to know. That wind was not easy. Irma had the sliding door dancing as if she wanted to push it in. I was dancing with it for a while. When I finally got a break, I pushed the big couch in front of it. Listen, at one point I thought it was going to just blow in. Boy, that wind had me on edge. I felt like I was sweating bullets."

"Yes, sah," her mom chimed in. "Sam and I were mopping water until we were tired."

Tianna's mom was referring to her dad when she said "Sam." His name was Samuellyn, but whenever anyone would ask him his name, he would say Samuellyn, then follow it with, "I'm such a small man, and they gave me such a big name. Just call me Sam."

As her brother and father inspected the damaged windows, they agreed to board up the house while they were there. They ventured outside and found three pieces of plywood that flew into the yard during the hurricane, as they were not there before.

The shorter piece of wood was used for the kitchen window. This did not cover the entire window, but it covered the damaged section. They proceeded to put it in place from the outside of the building, as it was at a level on which they could work.

Since there was no ladder available, they took the other two pieces of wood on the inside of the house, and with much communication that kept Tianna in giggles, her dad and brother accomplished the task as best they could. Tianna could not stop laughing even after they were finished. Her mom caught on with the giggles too.

"Not like that, Lee, you're hitting the nail wrong," her dad said.

"Give me a chance, Daddy. Just hold the wood straight."

"You see what I was telling you. The nail is bent," her dad hollered.

"Okay, since you're so good, you do it."

And so the conversation went, until the job was done.

"Not perfect, but that will do," Tianna quietly mumbled to herself as she looked at the number of nails that had been driven into her bedroom wall and the gaps between the wall and the wood.

Both men had worked hard. They were sweating buckets a drop when it was all done.

Before leaving, her brother asked if there was anything she wanted them to help her with before they left. She pointed to the rug that covered her living-room floor that was floating in water. He got everyone to help him move the couches so he could roll up the rug. He then dragged it out on her big lawn space and opened it up to be dried in the sun. Tianna thanked them several times. She was so grateful.

When they left, Tianna went back to her cell phone, took it apart, and put it on the table to dry out.

"Ms. Te," Joshua called when he returned to Tianna's house later that afternoon.

Her heart skipped a beat and an automatic smile covered her face. Her mind was on Joshua all day. Was his brother okay? Will he really come back to secure the front door? Did he notice she was into him?

I hope not, she thought.

She took a deep breath and headed to the front door area with its new feature—a ventilation system.

"Hi, you look okay. How is your brother?" she asked.

"He is good. His challenge is his wife."

"What about her?"

"She is really shaken up. They got hit hard. Just a small part of their roof is damaged, but almost all the windows upstairs and downstairs were blown in."

"Were they in the house at the time?"

"I went there and saw no one, so I was getting really concerned. There was almost nothing in the house. Doors were blown open or missing, the bed had no mattress, and no one was anywhere to be seen. It was not a pleasant sight."

"So did you eventually find them?"

"Yes. As I was coming down the hill, I saw her by the neighbor's house."

"You mean the neighbor just above me?"

"Yes! I saw her outside. When I asked her for my brother, I realized that she was crying."

"Crying?"

"She was trying to cover it up, but she eventually told me that she doesn't think she can stay here. She's taking it hard."

"It is a hard pill to swallow, but we can rebuild. What did you tell her?"

"Pretty much the same thing—we can rebuild 'cause as long as we have life, there is hope."

Tianna then went over to where she left her cell phone drying out.

"I found my cell phone in a pool of water," she shared.

"Is it working?"

"No, but I have taken it apart to dry out."

"Put it in some rice," he suggested. "How did it get in water?"

"That's a good question," she answered.

Joshua examined the damaged front door.

"Look," he said, "this door will have to be replaced. It was compromised in the areas where it needs the most strength. I will get one from the rubble so that you can have a door temporarily."

"Thanks, Joshua. That would be better than nothing."

With this, Joshua went behind the house where Irma had scattered the pieces of the place he once called home and got all the material he needed to secure Tianna's front door. He was also able to get her back door to "opening" status.

Tianna was preparing dinner. By the time Joshua was finished, she offered him something to eat and they sat down under candlelight. This made Joshua uneasy.

It took him back to a childhood memory. Very early one Good Friday morning, he was awaken to extreme panic. A neighbor's house was on fire. His dad ventured over to help while his mom kept her curious boys in her safe embrace. Many of the other neighbors were gathering to the scene as well. Some watched while others risked their lives to save the family who lived in the house. However, despite all the effort and sacrifices made, five-year-old Danyelle, one of his classmates, was trapped inside.

It was later revealed that a candle that was left burning throughout the night had started the fire. When Joshua heard this news, he was resigned to never having any dealings with candles. With that, he ensured that he would buy a flashlight for Tianna.

CHAPTER 10

The sun rose beautifully in the eastern sky on Friday morning.
When Tianna saw the light beaming through the living-room windows, she shouted, "Praise be unto your name, Lord God." She had said it three times before she remembered that she was not alone. She was just so accustomed to being by herself.

Joshua had accepted her offer for dinner the night before. After they were finished eating, they talked until Tianna fell asleep.

Tianna sprung from the couch. This was her "new" bed. In her quest to find out whether or not Joshua had left, she found him in the kitchen.

"Morning," she said, "You're up early. What are you doing here?"

"Morning, sunshine, you thought I walked home in the dark and violated the curfew?"

"No! I mean in the kitchen."

"Oh, I thought you wanted to get rid of me after our talk last night."

"What talk?" Tianna looked, disconcerted.

"You mean you slept it off that quickly?"

Tianna took a deep breath and held down her head.

"No, it's just—" She paused.

Joshua gently held her by both of her arms.

"Look at me," he said. Tianna took another deep breath before lifting her head and gazing into his enchanting eyes.

"I have searched my heart over and over, and I know you are the one for me. I want you in my life. If you need some time to think about it, it's okay. I can wait."

When he was done talking, he leaned over and kissed her on her forehead. She closed her eyes and took another deep breath.

"Are you all right?" he asked as he released her arms.

"Yes, thank you," she responded as she slowly moved away. "I need to use the bathroom."

When she got to the bathroom, she immediately closed the door, threw herself over the bathroom sink, turned the water on, and whispered, "Lord, I should only feel this way when I am in your presence. Father, please help me to keep my focus on you. Whenever Joshua is around, I don't want him to leave, but it makes me feel so . . . so weak. Right now I feel like my feet are about to fall off. Guide me, Lord. I commit this day into your capable hands! Amen."

"How is your hand?" Joshua hollered. "Are you going to the hospital today?"

"Geez, I hope I wasn't speaking loud enough for him to hear me," Tianna whispered to herself before answering.

She emerged from the bathroom holding up her left hand, which was now a lot fatter than her other hand.

"My hand has swollen a little more," she replied. "I think I'll go to the hospital later this morning."

"That sounds good. Since my brother's wife is not taking it very well, they are flying out this morning. I will have my brother's truck while he is away, so I will take them to the airport and come back to take you to the hospital."

"What time do they need to be at the airport?"

"Nine o'clock."

"What time is it now?"

"Six twenty-five."

"Well, maybe you should go check on them now to see how plans are going."

"Okay! When I get back, I'll take you to the hospital."

"I guess it is good for a lady to have a reliable handyman around at a time like this."

"Why did you say that?"

"Well, if I had a guy around, my windows would have been boarded up, and I would not have injured my hand."

"Why didn't you call me?"

"Someone had promised to do it, but he did not show up. It eventually got too late to call anyone."

"Give thanks. It could have been worse."

"That's true, but you know what? I will make sure that I get the traditional wooden shutters that don't need an exclusive expert to install. Then, I can open and close them myself. I have always liked them, and I feel that they are the most cost effective and reliable. They don't need electricity, and if a piece of debris loses its sense of direction and runs into it and it gets damaged, it would be easier to replace than other options, and almost guarantee that my windows would not get damaged, at least not as badly."

"Why didn't you get them before?"

"I was told to consider other options. When I did, it only cemented my desire to get the traditional shutters. I have procrastinated on getting them for too long that it cost me a hand and a cheekbone. I like them, and I will get them."

"Yes, ma'am."

As Joshua turned to leave, Tianna remembered how the day started.

"By the way," she said, "You didn't tell me what you were doing in the kitchen."

"I was going to make you some breakfast, but I could not figure out where you hide your dishes."

She laughed.

"Ah, that is so sweet. Are you sure you were looking with your eyes open," she said jokingly.

He looked at her with a smirk.

"I'll see you later," he said and left.

It was not just an ordinary ride to the hospital; it was also a sightseeing tour. The devastation they were witnessing was far beyond their comprehension. Big trees and poles were across the main road to Lambert, so they took the route through Parham Town, which was already clear.

With all the leafless trees, every house was in clear view. They saw houses they had never seen before, and some houses that once existed were just a memory and a vacant spot of land, or a pile of rubble.

They were both surprised to see the amount of people on the road. These persons were not just walking the street; they looked as though they all went shopping. Which shop could be open at this time without electricity, they wondered. They were soon to find out that those folks were looting. Some had a case of beer, cases of water, car oil, and everything they could get from the convenience store at the neighborhood gas station.

Heavy equipment operators were on the job clearing the road of fallen trees, poles, electrical wires, galvanize, and all kinds of household items.

As the "tour" continued, they saw huge trailers upside down; cars were in all kinds of amazing places—on their sides, upside down, in the hills, and even hanging over people's back walls. They were all over.

One of the side glasses had blown out of Joshua's brother's truck, but many of the vehicles persons were driving had multiple glasses missing. No one seemed to have a problem driving their once brand-new-looking vehicle.

One young man had a bus with all its glasses missing. The right side looked like something fell on it. Yet with one hand resting on the door and the other on the steering wheel, he was in the sightseeing line of motorists.

People were shouting to each other with the excitement of being alive and the desire to tell their survival story.

Tianna was taking pictures with her camera when Joshua noticed that she went quiet.

"Are you okay?" he asked.

When she did not answer, he took a good look at her and observed that her eyes were welled up with tears.

"What's wrong?" he inquired.

"I just can't believe this has happened. Look at all those houses without roofs. What will those people do? Not only do the houses have no roofs, but they all look empty. I am sure some people took years to acquire all that they had in their homes."

"Well! It may take years for them to get back all that they have lost, but we can now only take it one day at a time."

"I guess you're right," she said as she tried to regain her composure.

Upon arrival in Baughers Bay, there was a long line of vehicles on one side of the road. When they inquired, they were informed that the gas station in that area was open.

"I need to put some gas in the truck," Joshua said.

"Well, go ahead and join the line now before it gets longer," Tianna suggested.

"That would mean that you'd get to the hospital God alone knows when."

"I'll just catch a ride and meet you later."

"Later when? You don't have a phone that I can call you."

"I'll be fine. Just check on me later at the house since I don't know what time I'll get through at the hospital."

"Okay, be very careful. I'll see you later at the house."

"Thanks, Joshua!"

CHAPTER 11

"Nick, Nick," Tianna shouted.

A few minutes after she left Joshua in the truck, she saw a vehicle pass and recognized the license plate. It was her youngest brother. Fortunately for her, all the glasses on his jeep, except the windshield, had blown out, so he was able to hear her clearly.

"Morning! How are you?" she asked with the excitement of seeing him and not having to wait a long time to get a ride.

"I'm good you know. You?"

"I'm fantastic!" she exclaimed. "Alive and kicking."

"Where are you headed?"

"I'm going to the hospital to check on my hand."

"What happened to it?"

Tianna lifted her left hand for him to see its swollen state.

"Wow! That happened during the storm?"

She answered in the affirmative and proceeded to tell him the story.

"You know," he said, "I was going to get out of this line and take the other road, but I got the inspiration to stay, and I'm glad I did because I would not have seen you. How is your house?"

"A few windows blew out, the bedroom door blew off and the front door was severely damaged, but I'm thankful to still have a roof over my head. How did you and the family fare?"

"Te, that was not fun. The window in our bedroom blew out, so I went to close the door. When I felt that force of wind, we all hurried to the other bedroom."

"Who is 'we'?"

"Wifey, Rennie, and me."

Nick also called his wife Dee, as both of her names started with *D*. Rennie was their two-year-old daughter. There were also two teenagers between them who were spending time with other family members.

"How did Rennie feel?" Tianna inquired about her niece.

"She kept saying, 'Daddy I'm scared.'"

"What did you tell her?"

"'Daddy is scared too, but we'll be fine.'"

"So where are you headed?"

"Back to the house to start cleaning up."

"Where are you guys staying?"

"By a neighbor, but I'm ready to get back to my own space."

"I know exactly what you mean."

When they arrived at the hospital, Tianna checked in and took a seat as instructed. After she inquired about her position in the line and observed the process, she went in the parking lot, where Nick was waiting for her, and told him he could go ahead as she was uncertain how long it would take for her to be seen by a doctor.

Nick wanted to wait for her but agreed to go, as it was already eleven o'clock and he wanted to do some cleaning up to get back to his family before dark.

The hospital was not as crowded as Tianna had anticipated, but that did not mean it was not busy. There were people in other areas that she could not see. She had thought that she should just ask for a tetanus shot and be on her way. However, when she heard a nurse tell someone that the line for tetanus was long and that diabetics and emergency personnel were getting first preference, she decided to wait it out.

When she was eventually called, she was pleased—anxious to get checked and get out.

Her vitals were checked, recorded, and she was directed to a waiting room. Those in that particular area had already been checked and were ready to see the person that would address their particular issue.

There was an American couple. The pointer finger on the husband's right hand was almost severed. They were house-sitting the house in which they experienced the storm. While the husband seemed caught up in his injury, his wife told the story of how they were fighting with the front door when it closed in on her husband's finger. They immediately abandoned that assignment, and she nursed the finger as best she could until they could get to the hospital.

Getting to the hospital was a challenge all by itself, as their driveway was blocked, and they had to arrange to get it cleared so they could drive out.

One doctor took a look at the finger and said that it could not be stitched, on the basis that it was already a few days stale. Nevertheless, she took them away to have another look at it.

A police officer who was also in the waiting room shared that he had helped to clear the road to someone's house when the news spread that a part of the house had collapsed on the homeowner. He said that when they finally arrived, a couple days after the storm, they had to source heavy equipment to remove the debris from the deceased. He then shared that all was going well until he stepped on something that punctured his foot, so he was only there to get a tetanus shot. When he started to complain that he felt he was sitting there too long, another patient asked him if he had his vital checked. He responded that he was just sent to the area. A passing nurse was then alerted, as it was said that essential workers were being given priority. With this, he was ushered to another area for assistance.

Everyone had a story to tell. Tianna struck up a conversation with the lady sitting beside her, who was sitting next to another lady. They both had hand injuries and seemed as though they were related and had traveled together. There was an obvious age difference between them.

The conversation was interrupted when Tianna was called to get an x-ray done on her hand. When her process was complete, the ladies followed, one after the other.

A few minutes after returning to the waiting room, a doctor approached the older lady and told her that her hand was fractured and that someone would come to assist her to get it dressed. She then moved to Tianna and the younger lady and announced that they both had broken bones.

"A broken bone?" Tianna commented in surprise. That was the last possible news she expected to hear. First of all, she had never had a broken bone in her life, and secondly, it was not painful.

The doctor further explained that Tianna's middle finger was broken, which was another surprise because it was her ring finger that was hurting when touched. The other lady was informed that the bone in her forearm was broken, and she thought it would have been her wrist, as there is where she felt the most discomfort.

After the doctor shared her findings from the x-rays, she informed the ladies that they would have to get casts and asked them to follow her. As they were on their way, Tianna questioned the doctor about having her left cheekbone x-rayed as it had also been hit by the door. The doctor examined the area with her hand and said that the bone was not broken, as the swelling process would have continued. This information was enough to comfort Tianna and prevent her from worrying about her face.

One by one, the doctor affixed casts to the area of the broken bone of each of the ladies. They chatted, sharing their storm stories and asking the doctor questions. They even helped each other in the process.

"You know, we've been talking all this time, and I did not ask you your name. My name is Nyka. The other lady is my mom. Nice to meet you," she said.

"I'm Tianna Corrington. The pleasure is mine."

While Tianna thought a handshake would have been in order, she had to forgo that thought, as Nyka's right hand was now in a cast and her left hand was in a cast.

CHAPTER

It was dark when Tianna finally got home, after having to accept the incarceration of her left hand. Her heart skipped a beat at the first glance that someone was on her front porch. Then she realized it was Joshua. She was so excited to see him.

The driver of the mini-truck helped to take the two cases of water from the truck and handed them to Joshua as Tianna greeted him gleefully.

Joshua's greeting to the driver appeared a bit cold to Tianna, but she decided not to jump to any conclusions.

"Thanks for the ride," Tianna shouted as the vehicle drove off.

Tianna knew that if Joshua was upset with her, she was culpable. She knew she could have asked someone to use their phone and touch base with him. She just loved being free-spirited. Besides, the opportunity to do some sightseeing in the town area, since this was her first time in town since the hurricane passed, was just so fascinating that she figured she would explain everything to him when she got home.

"Are you okay?" she asked as Joshua hauled the two cases of water inside the house.

"I'm fine," he grunted.

Tianna watched as he walked away.

When she got to the door, after struggling with the heavy bag of groceries she had purchased, feeling crippled with the cast on her hand, she met Joshua on his way out of the house.

"So is that him?" he questioned with a seriousness on his face that she had never seen before.

"Him who? What are you talking about?"

"Is that why you haven't answered me? Because you are seeing someone else?"

"What? No. That's—"

He interrupted her. "You know what, I was here all afternoon waiting for you, wondering sick if you were okay. Then you show up after dark, after curfew, with some guy. See you. I'm going to my brother's house."

"Seriously?" was all she could say. She could not believe what she was hearing. He did not even give her a chance to explain. He did not even notice there was a cast on her hand. He did not even help her with the groceries.

Tianna turned on the light on her iPod to see the time.

"Gosh, it's only 11:42."

She had put away her groceries and boiled some water to take a warm bath before settling in to bed early. She munched on something here and there because she had no appetite after Joshua left. She could not even say a straight prayer without him bombarding her thoughts. She just wanted to go to sleep.

"Dear Lord," she prayed, "you know my heart. You know how I feel about Joshua. You know I care about him and genuinely desire the best for him. But, Lord, that behavior tonight is something that I don't know how to appreciate. He did not even ask me what happened that caused me to be late getting home. He just jumped to his own selfish conclusion. Father, if this is a behavior that I would have to live with if we ever get married, then provide me with a release right now. Nevertheless, not my will, but thine be done. Please grant your humble servant sweet sleep, I pray. In Jesus's name, amen."

Joshua paced the floor of his brother's kitchen.

"What did I do? What did I do?" he asked himself as he slapped the wall.

He was very concerned about letting Ms. Te out of his sight when he joined that long line for gas. It is not that she is unable to take care of herself, but he just wanted to protect her as he said he would.

After waiting for gas for almost three hours, he anxiously headed to the hospital to get her. He went to the reception area and was directed to the emergency section.

The assistant did not know Tianna, but he checked the log and realized that she was there. He proceeded to inquire about her whereabouts. He went wherever he was told she might have been, but she was nowhere to be seen.

Joshua's heart was pounding in his chest as he returned to the truck.

"I wonder where she could have gone," he questioned himself.

Tianna had not mentioned what her plans were after leaving the hospital, so he left the hospital and drove around town for a bit before heading to the hardware store. He needed a tool and a few other items to continue the work on his brother's house. Besides, just in case Tianna got home early, he wanted to be there to help her with whatever she needed, especially since she had damaged her hand.

When he got all that he needed, he returned to his brother's house and started to work. He got so deep into what he was doing that the time just seemed to have flown by. It was five fifteen when he looked at his watch.

He cleaned himself up and dashed down to Tianna's house.

"I hope she didn't damage her hand too badly," he said silently.

When he got to the house, it looked the same as it did when they left that morning. Nevertheless, he called and called, and there was no answer.

He again looked at the time on his phone and decided to sit on the front step and wait for her. All kinds of things were going through his mind. Is Ms. Te interested in him? Would they make a good couple? Would she be willing to go to the States to visit his mom and dad?

A passing vehicle startled Joshua. He did not even realize that he had fallen asleep. He grabbed his phone and looked at the time. It was after six o'clock and dark, and Tianna was not back.

I wonder where she could be. I hope she's okay.

His mind started wandering again.

I hope she's not with someone else while I'm here waiting on her. Memories of Mandy replayed in his mind.

Amanda was the most beautiful girl in the school. At least that is what Joshua thought of his grade 4 classmate whom he called Mandy. She was smart, witty, and very affable. He always admired her and was intentionally kind to her. Yet he never had the right chance to share his interest with her. However, the second semester was almost ending, and there was a big sports event at the school. Neither was participating, and thus he had an opportunity to sit next to her. That was it. Theirs was a love story that would certainly end with "happily ever after," or so he thought.

Contrary to Joshua's dreams, his princess had started becoming quite friendly with another boy later in their senior year in high school. Although she denied it, he would hear the stories. When he finally saw it for himself, he swore he would never love again.

CHAPTER 13

The sun had barely peeped over the horizon when Tianna opened her eyes to a new day.

She had left one window open, and the cool breeze came through. She was so comfortable that she decided to just lie in bed and say a prayer that was inspired by Bishop T. D. Jakes.

"Father, I declare that I have your favor today. I declare that I am strong and well able to fulfill my divine destiny. I know that you are fighting my battles for me, and I thank you for your Word says the battle is not mine, the battle is yours. Help me at all times to pull out my weapon of praise, my best praise, a praise that makes you smile.

"I declare that I am a victor and not a victim. Your Word says that I am more than a conqueror through him that loves me. Thank you for your amazing love.

"Your Word says that I am the head and not the tail, above and not beneath.

"I declare that by your stripes I am healed. I shall live and not die. I declare that you are restoring health unto me and that you would satisfy me with long life.

"I declare favor in my relationship with you, favor in my relationship with my son and family, favor in relationship with my friends, and favor in my business relationships.

"Lord, I thank you for causing me to be in the right place at the right time and for causing people to want to help me.

"Thank you, Lord, for blessing me with creativity and for causing me to make good decisions with a clear mind. Your Word says that you have not given us a spirit of fear, but of power, love, and a sound mind.

"Father, I claim Psalm 84:11, that you are blessing me with favor and honor, and no good thing will you withhold from me, for my walk is blameless in you.

"I claim Habakkuk 2:3; that my vision is for an appointed time, and though it may tarry, I will earnestly wait for it.

"I thank you for ordering my steps and for convicting me to think, focus, and meditate on that which is true, honest, just, pure, lovely, of a good report, praiseworthy, and virtuous.

"Your Word says that no man has seen, heard, or can even imagine the wonderful things that you have in store for those that love you. I want to tell you, Father, that I love you.

"Thank you, Lord, for loving me the way that you do, not because of who I am but because of whose I am—your child. I commit this day into your hands Father. In Jesus's name I pray, amen."

As soon as she said "amen," there was a knock at the door.

She could not believe her ears as she listened again.

"Morning, Ms. Te."

It was Joshua.

"Coming," she said, then whispered to herself, "What do you want, Mr. Joshua Payne?" rolling her eyes.

Half of her heart was excited to see him, and the other half wanted to be upset with him.

Tianna opened the door, stared Joshua in his eyes, said nothing, then turned around to go back into the house.

"Ms. Te," Joshua said as he dashed behind her, closing the door behind him.

When he caught up with her in the kitchen, he held her by the hand, and she spun around. Their eyes locked.

Holding her by both shoulders, he took a deep breath.

"Ms. Te, look. I'm so sorry for my behavior last night, so sorry. I was so darn selfish."

"Mmm," Tianna mumbled.

"Listen. Please forgive me. I promise I will never treat you like that again." He paused and sighed. "How is your hand?"

She held up her left hand, which now carried the extra weight of the cast which housed it.

"It's just fine," she said.

"Please don't be sarcastic."

"The doctor said that my middle finger is broken."

"Broken!" he exclaimed with deep concern. "How long are you expected to have the cast on your hand?"

"About four to six weeks."

"That means you'll have to rest that hand."

"Like I told you, it's not hurting. I'll be fine."

"That is beside the point. You don't have to be so stubborn. I will draw enough water for you to use each day, and whatever you need to wash, just put them in a bag, and I will wash them at my brother's house for you. He has a generator."

"I'm going to clean up this place and get into my new normal."

"Remember, your hand has to heal. Sit and I'll get a few buckets of water from the cistern. Then we'll make breakfast and go from there. How does that sound?"

Although it sounded like a good idea to Tianna's ears, her heart was having a difficult time with it. She had gotten so used to doing things for herself that the thought of being served, she realized, would take a lot of getting used to.

"Seems like your mom did a good job raising you. Or is it that she treated your dad like a king and you took particular notice?"

"Well, my parents only had boys, so I guess we got what the girls would have gotten."

"I guess you can wash and iron too."

"Whatever you can do, I can do better."

They both laughed.

"Whatever you say, Mr. Payne."

"Oh, and yes, my dad did treat my mom like a queen. That's what I want to do."

"What do you want to do?"

"Treat you like a queen."

With that Joshua kissed her on her forehead and walked off.

Tianna took a deep breath and sat down. Standing was never the position of convenience when Joshua was around, and that kissing her on the forehead was not helping.

Making breakfast together was most enjoyable for both of them. They talked about all kinds of things. They shared family traditions, as well as likes and dislikes in the kitchen.

When they sat down to eat, Tianna asked him to say the grace.

"Wow! I have not done that in so long," he said. "Nana always said to pray from your heart, so here goes . . . Hey, you have to close your eyes," he said as he observed Tianna staring at him.

"Okay," she responded, and closed her eyes.

He paused and looked at her with her eyes closed. *You are so beautiful*, he said in his mind.

She opened her eyes and startled him.

"Are you praying in silence?" she asked. "My breakfast is getting cold."

"No. Close your eyes."

"You close your eyes first."

"Okay."

He closed his eyes.

"Dear God, I thank you for life and for your loving kindness. I ask that you bless Ms. Te and bless this delicious breakfast that we're about to eat. It smells so good. Amen."

He hurriedly added, "Oh, and, Lord, heal Ms. Te's hand to perfection I pray. In Jesus's name, amen."

"Amen," Tianna declared. "Thank you for praying for my hand."

"Only because I truly care about you, Ms. Te."

They began to eat the meal they had prepared together.

"I was thinking that I would like you to meet my parents," Joshua said as he looked directly at Tianna to observe her first response.

"What?"

"I want you to meet my parents."

"Seriously?"

"Yes, seriously! Ms. Te, I know you are the one for me, and I don't want to lose you. Besides, if there is any doubt in my mind, my parents can help to clear it up." He gave a smirk.

"We barely know each other."

"Is that your biggest concern? Why do you think the vows say ''til death do us part'?"

"What is your interpretation?"

"Two people can be together for their entire life, and when one dies, they realize that they really did not know everything about that person."

"What are you saying?"

"We will have the rest of our lives to get to know each other. The only issue would be the will to love."

"You said you were a Christian. Where do you stand in your relationship with God?"

Joshua paused. Since he had asked Tianna about her faith in God during the passing of the hurricane and she responded with such confidence in the affirmative, it prompted him to start reading his Bible and praying.

"We have been in conversation. I am just not where you are, so please be patient with me."

"Sure."

They remained at the table and chatted for a few minutes when they were finished eating. Then Tianna rose up and started collecting the dishes to take to the sink.

"So do you forgive me, Ms. Te?"

Tianna looked deeply into his eyes for a few seconds. "Yes! I forgive you, and please stop calling me Ms. Te. You make me sound like I am an ol' granny walking around the house in a long frock with a head tie on my head, an oversized apron, and a cleaning cloth in my hand everywhere I go."

He opened his eyes wide, and a wide grin covered his face.

"Wow! That was very descriptive. It seems as though you watch too many classical movies. Or maybe you'll be a good writer someday."

"Whatever."

"So what do you want me to call you?"

"Te, Te," she quipped.

"Tit-tie?" he questioned with a mischievous smile and a gleam in his eyes.

"Keep your mind on the Lord, mister. You can call me Tia."

"Okay, now that sounds better. So what are your plans for today?"

"I would like to clean up this place as much as possible, throw out what is not needed or damaged, and create a new comfortable normal."

"Good. If you put all the clothes that you want to wash in a bag, I will go and wash those. When I get back, I will help you put the rugs in place, as they should be dry by now. Just be sure not to do anything that would jeopardize the healing process of your hand."

Joshua swept water from the floor while Tianna gathered the clothes in her closet that were wet and littered with debris and put them in a bag.

Sunday morning, Tianna got up early. She wanted an early start to go to Havers, which was on the other side of the island. Joshua had offered to drive her around to prevent a repeat of what happened just days before.

She needed to check on Ms. Snoyl's property. Ms. Snoyl was a motivational speaker who moved to Tortola from America. When she lived on the island, she hired Tianna as her executive assistant. However, when she left the island, Tianna took on the responsibility to manage her house.

A few months before the storm, new tenants had moved into the house. The brothers, who were from Guyana, were very uncomfortable with the thought of a category 5 hurricane, as they had never experienced a hurricane in their homeland.

Tianna and Joshua traversed along the Drakes Highway, which led to town, along the coastline of the island. When they got to Paraquita Bay, the rules for the motoring public had drastically changed from driving on the left side to driving on the best side. Every driver tried to avoid potholes that seemed like you would disappear if you fell into one. Some of the holes were filled with water so that every now and again, a driver would make a surprise drop into a big hole.

Although Tianna had not directly discussed introducing Joshua to her parents, she did have it in mind as her family meant the world to her.

"I'd like us to make a stop in Brandywine Bay," she proposed as they got near.

"Are we going to stay long?"

"A few minutes. I'm taking you to meet my mom and dad."

"Just like that?"

"What do you mean by 'just like that'?"

"Well, you should have given me a heads-up so that I could prepare myself."

"You look fine."

"I'm not talking about how I look. I mean being mentally prepared."

"You'll be just fine. Just be yourself."

"Do you think your mom and dad would like me?" he asked.

"Sure! Why not?"

This left Joshua deep in thought.

What would her parents think of me? Is it that she is truly that comfortable with me? This certainly looks like a good sign, he pondered to himself.

When they arrived at the house, her nephew was in the yard. He was her parents' first grandchild, Dee's firstborn. She greeted him warmly, as he always reciprocated the same level of greeting.

"Hi, Mother," she said with a smile as her mom opened the door after several knocks.

"Tianna," her mother answered back with a smile.

They hugged as Joshua stood in the background. Then her mom noticed him.

"Who are you?" her mother asked, gazing at Joshua.

"Mom, this is Joshua. He's with me. Is Dad home?"

"Yes. Come in and close the door quick from those mosquitoes that seem to want to take over the place."

"My sweet daddy, how are you?" she embraced her dad and planted a kiss on his cheek. To her he was a giant in a tiny framework. She loved him so much. He was always honest and candid whenever she would put any matter of concern to him. That just helped to draw her closer to him.

"I'm fine," he said with a grimace. He was still feeling some pain in his neck and about his body.

"So, Tianna, is that your boyfriend?" her mom questioned.

"Izzy, what are you asking the girl?" her dad said in her defense.

"I want to know who he is to her. I'm praying for her to meet the right guy, and I was wondering if he's the answer to my prayers."

"Even if that's the case, she would tell us when she's ready. Right, Te?"

"Yes, Dad," she responded.

"So, Mr. Joshua, what is your last name?" her mom continued to question regardless of what her husband had to say.

"Payne."

"That sounds like a Vincentian name. Where are you from?"

"St. Vincent."

"Which area?"

"Prospect."

"Oh, you're from the rich-people area. Tianna's father and I are from St. Vincent, but we have lived on Tortola before she was born," her mom reported. "Now this is home. As bad as the storm was, we have not even thought of leaving. We believe that together we can all rebuild."

For Tianna, the atmosphere got a little uncomfortable, so she decided it was time to go.

"I just came by to say hi and see how you guys were doing. Joshua is driving me around so I don't want to hold him up too much."

"Would you like something to drink?" her mother asked. "You can take it with you."

Even from a child, her mother would always ensure that she at least offered a drink to anyone that visited the house. Tianna concluded that that is the reason she liked Vitamalt (classic), because that was her mother's favorite drink and often the one she had to offer.

She asked Joshua if he wanted. After being served, they left with their cold drinks.

CHAPTER 14

There was silence in the truck for a few miles after Tianna and Joshua left Brandywine Bay.

"You seem awfully quiet," Tianna broke the silence.

"Your mom is really something else," Joshua responded.

"That's my mom."

"Would you be that way with your children?" Joshua said in jest.

This made Tianna's countenance change so that he was sorry he asked the question. She did not respond, and she looked in the opposite direction and said nothing for another few miles.

Joshua quietly wondered what he could have said to make Tia so uncomfortable. He decided he would ask her about it at a more convenient time. For now, he would just sightsee and enjoy the moment as best he could.

When they got to town, they were both surprised that the small wooden Craft Alive buildings were not damaged. Craft Alive is a village-like tourist area in Road Town, with tiny houses in all colors of the rainbow. Each was occupied by a vendor selling a variety of craft items and souvenirs, many of which were made by the vendors.

There was a ferryboat cocked on the shoreline, as if it was trying to escape being tossed about by the boisterous seawater.

Like other places, the town looked like so much was missing and buildings that once existed left vacant lots. There were even concrete buildings that just crumbled.

When they finally arrived at the house, Tianna could not believe her eyes.

"Oh my goodness! Oh my goodness!" Tianna shouted. She covered her mouth and looked at Joshua, her eyes filling up with tears.

"Wow, I feel so sorry for the owner," Joshua said.

"Oh my goodness, Ms. Snoyl is going to cry."

"Where is she?"

"She's in the States."

Tianna got out of the truck and stood in shock. Observing her, Joshua, too, got out of the truck and embraced her.

"Oh my goodness. I hope the tenants are okay," she said in a muffled voice.

Together they walked toward the building, stepping over the tall trees that had fallen across the driveway. The outside shed had blown open, and everything was scattered across the front of the house.

"How was the house designed?" Joshua inquired.

"There was a deck over there, and this area was the living room," Tianna said as she pointed to a pile of rubble. "This area was the dining room, and around here is the kitchen."

"What's behind this door across from the kitchen?"

"That's a bathroom."

Tianna opened the door to the half bath and peeped inside.

"Listen," she said, "I feel so uncomfortable in this building. It feels spooky, like it could crumble any minute. I'm going outside."

When they got outside, Tianna continued to describe the former look of the building.

"The area over the car park was a deck off the master bedroom. The wall for the master bedroom is gone. The wall that is still standing with the two door spaces—one door led to a full bathroom, which was also connected to the other bedroom, and the other door goes to a landing that took you from the master bedroom to the stairs."

"Well, the staircase looks like Irma was trying to make a highway to heaven," Joshua quipped.

Tianna gave a half smile. Although she did not feel like being humored, Joshua's comment helped to make her relax. She had always tried not to waste energy on things she could not change.

"I hope the tenants got down from there before she started working on it," Tianna said in response.

"I don't see any signs of blood or trauma, so I believe they are okay."

"I hope so."

"Do you have a camera to take some pictures to send to the owner?"

"Let me get it."

After taking a few pictures, the two continued sightseeing on the ride back to town. They encountered a long line of vehicles. The traffic was moving slow because of the cleanup work that was ongoing.

The stop they made in town was to see her sister Jan, who worked with one of the major insurance companies.

Tianna had not seen Jan since she returned from her vacation. She had heard that Jan did make it back, but nothing more.

The office was busy when Tianna and Joshua got there. The front desk assistant asked each person to briefly state what they each needed, and Tianna was ushered in to see Jan. Although Jan had a customer, when they saw each other, the sisters rushed into each other's welcoming embrace, as if they had not seen each other in years. Moments later, they released each other, and Jan asked Tianna about her hand. Tianna told her the story, which included the damages to the house.

"So you came to make a claim for your house?" Jan asked.

"Can you claim for your house if you had windows and doors damaged?" the customer asked as she was filling out a claim form for her vehicle.

"Yes," Jan replied. "You will get whatever is above your deductible."

"What is my deductible?" the customer further questioned.

"Two percent of the sum insured."

Jan then turned her attention back to Tianna.

"So how are you otherwise?" she asked her older sister.

"I'm giving thanks for life. When did you guys get back?"

"Thursday. Girl, I was so anxious to get home."

"So how are the bae-baes?" Tianna inquired of Jan's teenaged children.

Her son was older, and he had graduated from high school in June. Her daughter was promoted to her final year of high school. However, with the extensive damage to the school, the opening date was uncertain.

"They are good."

"This is Joshua Payne," Tianna announced when they finally got caught up on the updates.

"Girl! He is some eye candy. Where did you find him?"

"He is my former tenant."

With this Jan reached out her hand and pulled Joshua in her embrace.

"Remember, you're married," Tianna said with the caution of a big sister.

"Being married doesn't mean that I can't look. Haven't you ever been window shopping? You just look, you don't buy."

"Pleasure to meet you," Jan said as she shook his hand. "What did you say your name is?"

"Joshua. Joshua Payne."

"Ooo, your hands are soft. You don't do any hard work?"

"I'm a carpenter."

"Where are you from, Joshua Payne?"

"St. Vincent."

"Oh, so you a' one Vincy," Jan said, trying to speak like a Vincentian.

Jan then turned her attention to Tianna.

"Girl, don't let this one get away, you know."

"Listen, we have to go," Tianna said as she fixed her bag on her shoulder. She was beginning to feel a little uncomfortable, as she had not yet disclosed her true feelings to Joshua.

"Ms. Snoyl's house was destroyed, and I'm going to her insurance company to file a claim."

"Wait a minute? Did you say former tenant? What does that mean?" Jan questioned.

"My wooden house is no more."

"It blew down, completely?"

"Yes, girl."

"Not with him inside, I hope. Nah, he's too fine to get hurt," she questioned and answered herself.

"How is your house?" Tianna asked.

"A bedroom window blew out, and everything else in Irma's path ventured elsewhere, but I'm thanking the Almighty. You know my roof is concrete, so my bed is dry."

"Good for you, we have to run. See you."

"Okay, you all take care of each other."

With that they left the office, which seemed busier than when they first arrived.

CHAPTER 15

On Sunday, as usual, Tianna got ready for church after observing that there were ants marching around in her house. For her, this was a sign that Hurricane Josè had changed his mind.

Although she had not made contact with anyone to find out the status of the church services, she decided to go anyway. Joshua joined her.

When they got to the church, the upstairs was a complete mess. Many of the windows had blown in, and there was debris everywhere. Even some of the pews that were bolted to the ground could not withstand Irma's pressure. Some were bottom up.

The fellowship hall, which was on the ground floor, was nicely arranged. It looked like some sort of service was held. She spent a few minutes in prayer.

When she was about to leave, she saw the young man who was responsible for overseeing the premises. He informed her that service was held earlier and that everyone had already left. With this, she decided to go to the supermarket to get some groceries.

At about was ten thirty, there was already a long line of people at the supermarket waiting for it to open at noon. To Tianna, it felt like something out of a movie, something that happened to other people in other countries. Now it was her reality, and that of the residents of her beloved country.

Tianna did not like this kind of crowd, but decided that it was necessary to get a few essential items. Besides, the other option would put her in the same situation. Although the supermarkets did not open at the same time, they all had the same long-line situation.

The curfew was from six in the morning to six in the evening, so the opening hours of twelve to four was to give persons enough time to get their groceries and get home. In addition, Hurricane Maria was expected within the next few days, with category 2 strength winds.

Joshua had left her there and said he would return at noon when the supermarket was due to open. He went with a friend to help put a tarpaulin on the portion of his roof that had blown off.

From what he was told, it was not a very big area, so he decided he would have enough time to make a noticeable contribution and return.

Tianna was happy that she had her umbrella, as the sun was truly making its presence known, and it was going be a long wait.

While in the line, she tried to observe everyone around her. There was one lady just a few spaces ahead of her who just seemed to have a gloom-and-doom perspective to every matter that anyone spoke about. Everything was the government's fault, and she knew exactly what the government should and shouldn't be doing. Tianna eventually zoned her out, as her contributions to issues raised were not constructive.

Not long after standing in the line, a popular local saxophone player joined the line with his instrument and a bag strapped to his back. When he started to play, Tianna felt like she was really in paradise. The songs he played were just perfect and uplifting. He played oldies, newbies, gospel, R & B—a little from every genre, something that everyone can relate to.

There were several groups of persons surrounding Tianna. Many persons were sharing their "storm story." Tianna was not a part of any group; she just enjoyed the music. She did, however, observe that she was not the only one enjoying the music, as she saw a young lady that looked like she was in her teens bobbing her head and singing a few of the songs. The music provided such a ray of hope to the long wait. Tianna thought of how many persons have paid big bucks to hear this young man perform, and here they were, in a predicament, enjoying the blessings of his talent. A brighter day, she thought to herself, is on the way.

A little after noon, the crowd jolted forward. The store had finally opened its doors to the anxiously waiting crowd of people. However, only a few persons were being allowed inside at a time. In what seemed to be another half an hour before the line moved again, the lady that was now standing next to Tianna struck up a conversation with her. She had traveled to the island to work just eight months before the storm and was in a feeling of despair. Tianna was intentional about staying focused on all the things for which they each had to give thanks. Nevertheless, the lady shared her conviction that people will become desperate. She told the story of a friend of hers, whom she said was not a criminal and had not a criminal bone in his body, yet he was taking gas from someone's vehicle because he needed to get to work and the little money he had was running low. She told Tianna that he said it did not work because he's just not a criminal. They both laughed at his failed attempt.

"Well, as far as I know," Tianna said, "only a criminal engages in criminal activity. None of us is above the law, because we were all born in sin and shaped in iniquity. Suppose you were to find out that it was your employer's vehicle, how would that make you feel? Would you see that as a joke?"

Needless to say, the conversation ended there.

As the line moved along, Tianna realized that not everyone in the line was there to get groceries. There were persons standing along the side of the building charging their cell phones and other electronic devices.

What fascinated Tianna the most, however, was the ten-month-old baby girl in the line with her dad. He had put her in a shopping cart, in her car seat. She stayed there for the duration of the wait, looking up at everyone and smiling. She looked so peaceful that comments were being made that she is providing a ray of hope in the line.

Joshua returned to check on Tianna like he had said. The line was moving slowly, but she was nearer to the entrance by this time. He parked the truck and joined her in the line.

As she got closer to the door, Tianna was surprised to see persons she had met ahead in the line when she arrived, still in the line. She thought by now they would have already been preparing to leave the store. It turned out that there were persons who arrived just in time for the opening and joined the line at the door. They did not go to the back of the line like it was anticipated they would do.

Oh well, Tianna thought. There was no need to fuss about what she could not change, so she just kept quiet and waited for her chance to go into the supermarket.

Upon entering the supermarket, Tianna looked at the time; it was fourteen minutes after one o'clock. She looked around, observing the atmosphere and embracing the cool feeling of the air-conditioning after standing in the sun for two and three-quarter hours. She smiled to herself.

"This was worth the wait," she said to Joshua as he approached her with a shopping cart.

"What do you mean?"

"The air is cool, the atmosphere is pleasant, the smell of bread baking is warming, and the stalls are well stocked with food."

"What were you expecting?"

"With the line being so long, I was thinking that everyone who went ahead would get as much as they could in the midst of uncertainty. I guess I was really thinking scarcity."

"That goes to show that we should keep hope alive, regardless of how things look."

"Yep, you're right."

As they shopped, Tianna kept asking Joshua what he would like. She had gotten so used to his company at mealtime that it just came natural for her to have what he liked available for him.

They met a few of their friends and introduced each other. Everyone was just embracing the opportunity to tell their storm story to anyone who was willing to listen.

"Do you need batteries?" Joshua asked Tianna as he packed the groceries that the cashier had already cashed.

"They are completely out of the size D batteries," Tianna replied. "That's one of the first things I looked for."

As they drove home, Tianna reflected on her own experience with Hurricane Irma.

"Are you going to your brother's house tonight?" she asked Joshua.

"Right now that's the only home I have. Why?"

"After that Hurricane Irma experience, I don't think I want to be alone for Hurricane Maria."

"Are you trying to ask me to keep you company?"

"Something like that."

Tianna was not always as frank as she knew she should be, but it was definitely a place she aspired to get to.

"Something like that, or is it that?" Joshua asked, requiring clarity.

"Yes, it's that."

"Okay, that's no problem. I will be alone in my brother's house anyway," he responded. "I will drop you off, go to secure his house since Maria is now a cat 3, and come by you."

"A cat 3? Lord help us!"

CHAPTER 16

The wind was roaring on the outside when Tianna awoke on Tuesday morning. It was as if Irma had sent Maria with the same vengeance to finish what she had started.

Tianna got up and looked outside. She could not see Virgin Gorda and could barely see the airport. These were the markers she used for the nature of the weather for each day.

Joshua got up before Tianna and started making breakfast. Although Tianna was not used to such service and she preferred to serve rather and to be served, it did make her feel special awaking to breakfast already prepared. When they sat down to eat, they went back and forth for a few minutes about who should say the grace. Tianna eventually conceded and got carried away praying for peace in the midst of the storm and everything else that came to her mind.

When she finally opened her eyes, she did not immediately notice that some of the contents of her plate were missing.

"That was a good prayer," Joshua said as he sipped on his green tea with mint, trying not to look culpable.

"Wait a minute, mister," Tianna said as she picked up her fork and observed the disparity in her breakfast. "Did you exchange reverence for robbery?"

"What are you talking about? Aren't we expected to *watch and pray*?" Joshua asked, trying to keep a straight face.

"So while I was praying, you were watching my breakfast?"

"Actually, seeing that you have one hand to work with, I figured that I should cut everything into smaller pieces for you," he said with a sly look on his face.

"Don't try to butter me up."

"Butter you up? Hmmm, that sound appetizing," he said wryly.

"Let's just eat," she said, feeling that this conversation could go on and on without a purpose.

When they were both finished eating breakfast, they did the dishes and cleaned up the kitchen together. Tianna could not help but think that God surely must have spent a little more time on this one. He cooked and cleaned too.

"You are a keeper," she said.

This startled Joshua, who was deep in thought as he cleaned the stove.

"What? What do you mean?"

"No woman should let you go. You cook and clean too. Your mom deserves a medal."

"You know, I was just thinking of how much I hated to clean up and do the dishes when I was young. It always seemed that I was on kitchen duty when everyone else was having fun. But doing it with you just feels so . . . so right."

Joshua wiped his hand as he put down the dishcloth and pulled Tianna to him.

"Ms. Te—sorry, Tia, you have added so much value to my life already. I don't—"

Before he could finish the sentence, a thunder crashed so loudly, it was as if a huge boulder rolled from the heavens and had hit earth.

Tianna screamed and jumped closer to Joshua. She hid her face in his chest as if she had seen the boulder.

"Okay, that's it, I just want to go to sleep," she exclaimed.

"Go to sleep?" Joshua said, disconcerted.

"I really don't want to hear all that excitement going on outside."

The wind had started howling violently, not quite like Hurricane Irma, but with each heavy gust, the sound of windows bursting replayed in Tianna's mind.

She released herself from Joshua's embrace and asked him to put one of the couches in the kitchen.

"Why?" he questioned.

"I don't want to see the lightning, and if any of those windows blow out, or the door blows off, I think behind this wall in the kitchen will be a very safe place.

"All will be well, oh ye of little faith."

"Faith without works is dead," she fired back.

They both laughed.

When the couch was positioned exactly as Tianna wanted it, she curled up to fit and covered herself from head to toe.

"Just like that?" Joshua asked, feeling abandoned.

"Sorry, but I just want to go sleep so I won't have to hear all that excitement out there. Make yourself comfortable."

"Where?"

"In the other couch, or in my bed in the bedroom."

"You know what? I agreed to keep you company, so I'll be right here in the couch when you need me.

"Thanks, Joshua," the muffled voice sounded from under the covers.

Tianna did not know when she had fallen asleep. It seemed as though morning had come quickly. The wind was still packing high strength. Tianna removed the cover and called for Joshua, who was reading a book. He promptly went to the couch and sat beside her.

"I can't get back to sleep," she said.

"What do you want me to do?"

"Lay there."

"Behind of you?"

"Yes, please. Just lie down."

He obeyed.

Tianna nestled herself comfortably. She could feel the warmth of his body next to hers. It made her feel protected and relaxed. Joshua placed his hand around her waist. She embraced it and soon fell asleep.

Suddenly, there was another loud crashing thunder. Tianna jumped. When she opened her eyes, she realized that she was dreaming. She looked over at Joshua, and he was sound asleep.

"How can he sleep in all this?" she murmured.

"Lord," she prayed, "this whole hurricane story is really testing my faith. Your Word says that you have not given us a spirit of fear, but of power, love, and of a sound mind. Give me a sound mind and grant me a peace that passes all my understanding."

Just then, Joshua turned and opened his eyes.

"Are you okay?" he asked, with concern written all over his face.

"I will be."

With this, she covered herself and fell asleep.

CHAPTER 17

In the days following Hurricane Maria, everyone was forced to create and settle into a new normal.

The country embarked upon a massive cleanup campaign. Young men and women joined groups in different villages to help with the gathering and picking up of debris. Galvanize was just about everywhere and needed to be gathered to prevent unnecessary hazards. Fallen trees and poles had to be cut into pieces, and the road had to be made passable.

There were military personnel from the UK providing assistance with fallen poles and clearing public passageways. Property owners piled up their debris in central areas within their village where they could be picked up and disposed of by the designated crew.

The electricity corporation had locals, as well as volunteers from abroad, on board with them to assist with the restoration of the electricity supply. Tianna saw a visiting crew of electricity workers from VINLEC, the electricity corporation from St. Vincent and the Grenadines. This was particularly fascinating to her, as her roots were *planted* in St. Vincent. When she mentioned seeing the guys from VINLEC, she was informed that there were crews visiting from Canada, Turks and Caicos, Jamaica, St. Lucia, and many other countries.

Community centers in the different districts were providing members of their constituents with food and other essential items. Tianna went by once and received some items that were very helpful. However, she was most pleased with the solar light that she was given. For a long time, she had been trying to get some size D batteries. There was none in stock at any of the shops that would usually have them.

With her solar light, she could do a little work on her book, along with other chores. During the day, she would put it on her porch, in the sun, to charge.

Due to the fact that the electricity was off, she would ensure that everything she needed to do at her house was done before sunset. When it got dark, she would go to bed very early.

The thing she found most fascinating of all, though, was the fact that although there were many trees that had fallen flat on the ground, like one of her oleander trees, they were now sprouting new leaves, new life, renewed hope.

Whenever she saw that, she would say, "Knocked down, but not knocked out."

Days after Hurricane Irma, Joshua had heard that one of the ferries that he traveled on to go to work went missing, and the other was damaged. He was told that work would not begin again until the New Year.

On the basis that he now had time on his hands, he decided he would go fishing. As a boy, his dad took him and his brothers fishing in his small boat. There were times when the sea was rough and the waves would be so high that they could see the fish in the waves. Sometimes it even covered the boat. Joshua never liked the high-wave experiences, but he loved fishing.

One morning, Tianna did not see Joshua, and she did not hear from him for most of the day. She had gotten accustomed to him stopping by early in the morning to fill up the buckets with water and help with other things around the house. She did have enough water for that day, so she was okay in that regard, but still a bit worried about not seeing him.

However, later that day, there was a knock on the door. When Tianna opened it, she was surprised and excited to see Joshua.

"I was beginning to think that Irma or Maria came back and went with you," she greeted him.

"Now why would you say that?" he asked curiously.

"I got accustomed to seeing you early in the morning, and I did not see you this morning."

"I went fishing."

"You went fishing! Why didn't you invite me?"

"Would you have come?"

"Sure!"

"Oh, okay. My mom never liked going fishing with us, so I just figured it was a lady's thing to not want to join in such an activity."

"Next time don't assume," she advised. "So what did you catch?"

"These."

"Whelks? You took a bag with line, hooks, and sinkers to catch whelks? Who catches whelks with a line?"

"Don't be silly. The fish were not biting, so I saw whelks and got them. The thing is, I don't like whelks. Do you?"

"Of course, and right now they are a delicacy. I will boil them in some saltwater right now. Then I'll clean them and eat them."

Tianna took the whelks to the kitchen to prepare this delicacy that brought back fond memories of her childhood. She recalled going to pick whelks with her mom. It made her smile.

Joshua pulled out a chair at the table in the kitchen and sat.

"With all this time on my hands," he said, "I am planning to go visit my parents for a week. Would you care to join me?"

Tianna's mouth fell open, and for a moment she froze in place.

"Are you serious?" she said when she finally found her voice.

"I'll give you a couple days to make up your mind," Joshua said as he got up and went closer to her. "I want to leave this weekend."

"Geez, I would need more time to think about it."

"Don't think too hard," he said and kissed her on her forehead. "I am sure my mom would like you just as much as I do."

With that, he gathered his fishing gear, said goodbye, and went to his brother's house.

Later that night, with the thought that Joshua suggested that she join him to visit his parents, Tianna could not sleep. In addition, he wanted to leave on the weekend. She tossed and turned almost all night.

At that time, she was not working as all the places to which she provided a service, were destroyed by Hurricane Irma. Besides, she was incapacitated with a cast on her hand. There was no reason for her to turn down Joshua's offer.

She prayed, however, like Gideon in the Bible, and asked the Lord to show her a sign regarding her feelings for Joshua. If her heart felt reserved when she met Joshua's parents, she would know to run the other way. If she felt she knew them all her life and they embraced her like family, that would signal confirmation of the connection with Joshua.

Joshua's bold suggestion for her to meet his parents got her thinking that he could seriously be considering marriage.

Although she had thought about getting married with great excitement, the thought that it could actually be close to becoming reality was making her real nervous. Was she truly ready to give up her *freedom*? Would she add enough value to his life that would enable him to live out his purpose? Would he continue to help with the cooking and cleaning? So many questions went through her mind.

A few days passed, and she kept getting more and more excited about the trip, although she had not yet answered Joshua.

She had been to the United States many years before. It was in Miami that she had surgery on her eye to remove the damaged lens and reattach the retina. Then more than ten years later, she returned to Pennsylvania for her aunt's wedding, where she sang a solo.

It did not matter where she was going, Tianna loved to travel. Her employment with a motivational speaker afforded her the opportunity to travel to many of the Caribbean islands. She looked forward to someday visiting Dominica, St. Lucia, and Grenada.

She now figured that traveling with Joshua would give her an opportunity to get to know him outside of the posthurricane-adjusted life on Tortola.

Joshua had given Tianna time to think about taking the trip with him. He had not brought it up because he did not want her to feel that he was bombarding her. If she said yes, he wanted it to be of her free will, as much as he always wanted to have her around him.

"Tia, have you made up your mind about taking the trip with me?" he asked when he finally brought it up again.

She paused.

His heart started pounding as if it would jump out of his chest.

"Well . . . yes," she said.

"Oh great!" He jumped to his feet from where he was sitting at her kitchen table, picked her up, and spun her around.

She screamed. "What is wrong with you?" she asked.

"You have just made me one happy man."

"It's just a trip!"

"Well, actually, when I went to get the tickets, I got a deal I could not refuse, and with a deep conviction in my heart that you would say yes, I took the risk and booked a flight for you as well. Wait till I tell my mom you're coming with me."

"You are a mess, Mr. Payne."

"Thank you, Tia. Thank you for making this dream a reality. I will certainly have sweet dreams tonight."

"Just keep your mind on the Lord."

"Most definitely! I have to give him a personal thank-you."

CHAPTER 18

Tianna felt so refreshed after she returned from visiting Joshua's parents. They were both adorable, and Joshua was a great host.

She did not realize how uptight she was after those hurricanes and how much she needed to get away and relax.

The trip did so many wonderful things for Tianna. First of all, it helped her to cement her feelings for Joshua. She had questioned herself about being infatuated with him. Now she was sure that her heart would say yes to him without a question.

When they arrived, Ms. Jenny was very clear about the rules of the house and her expectations of them. She showed them to their separate rooms and gave them each a lecture about chastity.

One evening as Ms. Jenny, Joshua's mom, lay in her bed, she called Tianna. The two chatted and bonded. This gave Tianna the opportunity to share in Joshua's upbringing. His mother shared much about her own upbringing and why she insisted on teaching her sons the principles that she instilled in them.

As they lay on the bed like girlfriends from high school, Ms. Jenny shared that she was not accepted by her husband's mother, so she made up her mind to be the best mother-in-law she could to the ladies her sons brought home. She said that she was confident that her sons would choose wisely based on the principles they were taught.

Tianna got a firsthand feel for how much family meant to Joshua and how he valued his parents. It was no wonder he was so diligent in helping his brother rebuild his house.

When it came to family, Tianna too would act first and think later. Regardless of what any of her family members was facing, if she could help she would. As a matter of fact, she would even dare to put her job on hold to assist a family member in need.

At events of celebrations such as graduations and recitals, Tianna's mouth would be the loudest in the crowd when a family member was in the spotlight. She felt that every accomplishment should be celebrated in grand style, and setbacks should not cause separation.

The older woman had good house-fashion sense. She was a wonderful cook and had become a good friend and mother to Tianna.

The highlight of her trip, however, was at church on Sunday. Joshua's parents were dressed in matching colors. They led the way to the Sunday-morning service. They were great role models.

"I like this atmosphere," Tianna whispered to Joshua.

Joshua motioned in response but said nothing. In addition to the fact that he had started reading his Bible again, he prayed constantly for guidance, especially regarding Tianna and their growing relationship.

This morning, however, the presence of the Lord was very overwhelming as he entered the door. For a moment, he had forgotten that Tianna was beside him, until she whispered something that he did not understand.

The worship service was just heavenly. Song after song seemed to have been selected by God himself just for Joshua, or so he thought.

When it was time for the sermon, the preacher was introduced as a visiting pastor. He was tall and had a bald head, as shiny as could be. As he moved to the pulpit, Joshua's mind drifted to a T-shirt he once saw that read, "God only made a few perfect heads, on the rest he put hair."

Joshua chuckled to himself. Tianna perked him in his side and asked him what happened, but he just shook his head.

The topic of the sermon was "Living a Kingdom Life," and the text was taken from Romans 14:17–19. He started out by explaining an earthly kingdom in very descriptive detail, outlining who is there, the nature of what is there, in terms of value and available services, what is expected, the rules and regulations, and the authority of the head. He then aligned his foundation with God and his kingdom and used very relevant Scripture references, dissecting each one and bringing it down to where a child could understand. As a matter of fact, it seemed as though everyone in attendance was attentive to the sermon, even the youngest child.

The sermon ended with these questions: Are you a part of God's kingdom? If so, are others being influenced by your royalty? Do your words and lifestyle reflect kingdom standards? If not, you're in the right place at the right time. Now is your chance to declare your kingdom citizenship. Today is your day to begin living a kingdom lifestyle.

When the pastor was finished, the entire congregation stood in applause, with some moving forward to the altar for prayer.

Joshua did not know what came over him. He found himself at the altar crying out to God. He wanted to ensure that his citizenship to God's kingdom was secured. It was a life-changing moment for him.

Later that week, Joshua took Tianna to his favorite restaurant for dinner. It was two hours away from his parents' house. Tianna loved it. They talked and laughed all the way. There was never a dull moment.

Lenny was the host on duty that night. When they arrived, Joshua and Lenny greeted each other like they were friends from childhood, making all kinds of silly gestures and laughing. They had only known each other for a few years when Joshua started frequenting the restaurant whenever he would visit his parents. The two caught up for a bit until Joshua drew Tianna closer to him and introduced her as his lady.

"Wow!" exclaimed Lenny, "I have never seen him with a lady before. You must be very special." He reached out his hand. "I'm Lenny," he said. "It's such a pleasure to meet you."

"I'm Tianna. The pleasure is all mine," she responded with a smile.

Lenny led them to a seat for two in a corner, per Joshua's reservation request.

The lighting was just right. The air was cool and comfortable enough for Tianna's sleeveless elegantly casual floor-length dress, and although the restaurant was almost full, it was quiet enough to hear the soft instrumental music playing overhead.

They both ordered a glass of wine. She ordered white, and he got red.

When the drinks arrived, Joshua promptly lifted his glass.

"A toast," he said.

Tianna lifted her glass.

"To Irma!" Joshua declared.

"To Irma?" Tianna said softly, with a puzzled look on her face.

"Yes! Thank God for Hurricane Irma. She blew us together. And thank you for being so kind and patient with me."

"Oh, Joshua." Tianna blushed. "You have become so special to me. This all just feels like a dream that I don't want to wake out of."

"So to us?"

"Yes, to us!" Tianna responded in agreement.

Their appetizers were served not long after.

"Tia, I have something very important to tell you."

"Okay," she said, her mind racing, wondering what it could be.

"I've rededicated my life to the Lord," he shared.

She covered her mouth in pure excitement, wanting to cry and laugh at the same time.

"Really! Praise the Lord! I'm so happy for you."

She reached out her hands and gave him a clumsy hug from across the table. She did notice a change in him since Sunday's service.

"Now I will need you to be more patient with me and to help me stay focused."

"I hope you did not do it just because of me."

"Honestly," he said, "it is something I had been contemplating on for a very long time. You just helped me to put the nail in the coffin."

"I'm truly happy for you."

Moments later Tianna cleared her throat.

"Now I have three things that I need to tell you."

"One," he said, as if asked to keep count.

"I have an adult son."

"You do? Where is he?"

"He got mixed up in a situation and is now at a behavioral health facility in the UK."

"So is that his room behind that closed door in your house?"

"Yes. His situation breaks my heart so much that I just keep the room clean and pray for his restoration and return to a productive life."

"Have you visited him since he's been there?"

"No, but I'm scheduled to do so soon."

"I'd be happy to join you if you don't mind."

"Seriously? That would be truly, truly appreciated," she said, feeling a bit solemn as she reflected on her son being miles away.

Joshua reached for her hand and gave it a reassuring squeeze. He then leaned back in his chair and allowed her to catch herself.

"How long has he been there?"

"Three months."

"Do you know what happened?"

"Not exactly, but his behavior changed from loving and responsible to very, very weird. He stopped leaving the house, but if anyone visited the house, *if* he left his room to see them, he would appear very normal. To me, especially late night, it was a totally different situation. It was taking a toll on me to a point where I started sleeping with a stick under my bed. I hated that feeling so much. He is my only child, and the last thing I want to do is hurt him."

"How do you think you would feel when you visit him?"

"I'm not sure. It would be really nice to have you there with me because my heart hurts just wondering how he feels about me forcing him to the doctor's care."

"I am sure they can help him better than you can. What you did is a demonstration of your strength, as a mother. It will all be for the better," Joshua said as he again squeezed her hand to reassure her of his support.

A few minutes passed, and Tianna took a deep breath.

"Remember I told you that my eye was damaged in a car accident a few months after I graduated from high school? Well, there is a one in one millionth chance that the other one could be adversely affected."

"Can you see now?"

"Sure!"

"Well, while you can see, you have a choice to live life to its fullest, and if you fall in the one in one millionth category, we'll just deal with that accordingly. Three?"

Tianna looked at him with a smirk on her face.

"I'm an ex-con. As a matter of fact, the house you were living in was built out of the need for somewhere to live because my house was rented at the time."

"You were homeless? What happened to your family?"

"Well, I was living with a family member and that arrangement ran out of juice real quick. I was forced to find somewhere to live. The challenge is that I was not making enough money at the time to rent an apartment. So a gentleman whom I met after my release suggested that I build a small house on the top section of the land."

"You said you were not earning enough to rent an apartment. How then could you finance a small house?" Joshua asked curiously.

"Well, I spent a lot of time helping him with his business, so he used his influence to get a credit for the material needed. Then he got a guy that he knew to build it to where I could live in it. Thereafter, I took my time to work on it little by little, along with help from my son."

"So why didn't he finish what was started?"

"We fell out along the way."

"You know, I did hear about that journey."

"Really?"

"Yes. A coworker kindly informed me, when he saw us together. What I would like to know, though, and you don't have to answer, is, what was the experience like?" Joshua inquired.

"Of course no one wants to know that their name would forever be tainted by a stint in prison. Society tends to always remember and refer to that particular phase of one's life, no matter how well they have been restored. However, when I got there, I quickly accepted the fact that there was nothing I could do to change the situation at that point, so I embarked on an alternative mind-set. I read extensively, I ensured that I maintained my exercise routine, and I made a variety of craft items. I crocheted cushions, and even learned to knit with the two long pins."

"Wait a minute, people still do that? My grandmother made some nice blankets and other fancy things with those two pins. It looked so complicated to me," Joshua shared.

"There was a lady from Peru. She and I became good friends, and she taught me to knit. I made a couple hats with the matching scarf. We even did some baking. She told me she was a pastry chef, so I suggested that we make something together. We did get permission and one day decided to make bread pudding with some bread that was available. In the process, I noticed that the bread had ants, so I brought it to her attention. She said, as if proud of herself, 'Pan con hormigas.'"

"What does that mean?" Joshua asked.

"Bread with ants."

"What? You made bread pudding with ants?"

"Yup! And they were very delicious too," Tianna assured him as she acted out licking her fingers.

"Well, I guess what doesn't kill fattens," Joshua conceded.

They both giggled like teenagers.

"You know," Tianna continued with her report, "I went to court a couple times during my tenure in that place, and I made the outfits I wore. As a matter of fact, almost every weekend when I had a visit, I wore a new outfit that I made."

"You took your sewing machine with you?"

"I didn't have to. Apparently someone had donated a few of them—for my convenience! Ha-ha!"

"Sounds like you really made yourself at home."

"I have decided that whatever state I am, I would make myself comfortable. I was so comfortable that I wrote numerous poems. I even got a *second-place award* for a poem I wrote for an Arbor Day competition while in prison.

"I wrote one for a Spanish lady when she was about to leave. I included some Spanish that I asked another Spanish lady to translate for me. When I read the poem to her, she started to cry."

"You write poetry too? What can't you do?"

"I can do all things through Christ who strengthens me."

"Then I look forward to you writing a poem for me."

"I only write poems when I am inspired."

"Hopefully I can inspire you enough to write a poem for me. I love you so much."

Tianna blushed.

So what is your position on that?"

"First of all, you said 'ex-con.' To me, that means that you are no longer a con. There are a lot of people who are cons in so many ways, but they walk around looking squeaky clean. No one discriminates against them.

"Secondly, I believe that prison is 80 percent mental and 20 percent physical. There are a number of persons who are incarcerated in a relationship, at their place of employment, or in some other way. You have done your time, and as long as you are free within, I will always be your biggest fan as a great overcomer."

"Aw, thank you, Joshua. I feel like crying."

Joshua looked around the crowded room.

"You are free to express yourself, but I don't want these people to think that I am over here quietly hurting your feelings."

A big smile came over Tianna's face.

"Besides," Joshua continued, "a good friend of mine received his doctorate in theology while in prison. Today, he is a preacher and has a company that serves his community well. He is a kind and generous person.

"It is up to you to rewrite the script of your life through your attitude and lifestyle. Never give anyone the privilege to dictate who you are. My mom always told me, 'What others think of you has nothing to do with you. What you think of yourself is the ultimate truth.'"

When he was finished, Tianna's eyes were glistening with tears.

"Wow! That was a good sermonette, Pastor Payne."

They looked at each other, and after a second of silence, they both burst out in a hearty laughter.

CHAPTER 19

Six months later

Joshua had been trying to identify the best day and place to propose to Tianna. He wanted to factor in her family, as he knew how much they meant to her.

During his trip to visit his parents, he had told his dad of his intentions to propose to Tianna.

"Follow your heart," his dad first responded.

It was a saying that his dad would use whenever he asked for advice. He always found it to be words of wisdom because whenever he followed his heart, he always got a favorable outcome. If ever he was unclear about a decision, his dad would question him until he was clear on what he should do, even though he didn't do it at times.

Joshua decided to contact Dee, as Tianna had often shared how much they had in common. While Tianna was the one who would ensure that everybody's special event was celebrated, Dee was her point of contact for efficiency and effectiveness in executing each event.

Dee was the one who had planned Tianna's fortieth birthday party just as she envisioned it, with so many pleasant bonuses. She certainly pulled out all the stops, according to Tianna's report of the event.

Joshua ensured that the list of invitees for the engagement party included a few members of the church, as Tianna was a long-standing member, and from what Joshua observed, she was loved, and she made it a point to show love to all as much as possible. He had to find a way to pick her mouth to find out whom she would like to attend.

The day of the event had finally arrived.

As Joshua got ready for work early that morning, he wondered if Tianna had any idea of his plans and how she would react. He duly remembered that Dee had done all the hard work putting things in place so that he did not have to worry about anything. Working with Dee was one of the best working relationships he had ever encountered. She was so professional. She made him feel as if she could read his mind. Before he could think of an important factor, she would call to get his opinion on it and would keep him abreast on how things were coming together.

He had started working again. The first few months were just to clean up. Thus, he decided to make sure to take the day off. This would give him enough time to put some last-minute details in place.

His phone rang, and the caller ID showed that it was Dee.

"Hello," he answered.

"Good morning," she responded. "I have one last question. I want to make sure I get this right. Do you want the music to start playing after your brother comes in so that the door is clear before you come in?"

"Yes. I will come in on the first line. I don't want too much of a long pause before I am to enter. I don't want to be outside too long getting cold sweat."

"You'll be just fine. Just leave the cold sweat to my sister."

"Do you think she'll be surprised?" he asked with a little apprehension in his voice.

"Yes."

"Thanks for everything."

"No problem. See you later."

As soon as she hung up from speaking with Joshua, Dee heard a knock at the door. It made her jump. Then she looked at the time.

"That must be Tianna," she muttered. "She's always the first to show up at family gatherings."

Tianna was holding a cake that she had baked for the event. She handed the cake to Dee, who had told her that she would decorate it.

"So is Joshua coming?" Dee asked.

"He was planning to come, but something came up, and he has to work late."

"He'll miss the photoshoot."

"Photoshoot? Who is taking pictures?"

"Nick."

"You asked Nick to take pictures?"

"Yes! We do need some fresh family pictures."

The event was to be held in Lee's apartment, so Dee got Tianna to take the treats she had prepared upstairs.

When Tianna got upstairs, Nick immediately took a picture of her, which caught her off guard.

"Hey, I was not ready," she protested.

Nick had already arrived with his family. For a brief moment, Tianna thought this to be strange, as they were usually the last ones to attend family gatherings. Nevertheless, it was just good to see them. Just before Hurricane Irma, Nick had ventured into full-time employment for his photography business. He took every gig seriously.

Rennie, Nick's two-year-old daughter, ran to Tianna and greeted her with a big embrace. Tianna lifted her off the ground and gave her a kiss.

Lee's wife came on the scene just in time to retrieve the items Tianna held in her hand and took them to the kitchen.

When all the confirmed invitees arrived and were gathered downstairs in Dee's apartment, she got the ball rolling. She telephoned Lee's wife and made sure that Tianna was preoccupied.

Moments later, as Tianna sat on the couch, her mom and dad entered the room.

"Surprise," they said in unison.

Tianna immediately rose to greet them with a big grin on her face, always happy to see them.

As soon as she was done hugging her mom and dad, her sister Jan and her family entered the room and said, "Surprise." She hugged Jan. It was indeed a bit of a surprise to see Jan's husband, as it was a while since he had attended a family gathering. In addition, since her children started hitting their later teen years, they too were seen less and less at family gatherings. Yet she was getting a little confused about everyone saying "surprise" as they entered.

By the time she was finished hugging Jan and her family, Dee and her household entered and said, "Surprise."

"What's up with this 'surprise' thing?" she questioned in sheer confusion. "Mom and Dad said 'surprise,' and everyone is following them with this 'surprise' thing."

In addition to the fact that no one responded to her inquiry, everything was moving so fast that there was no time to stop for an answer.

When Gracie and her family entered and said, "Surprise," Tianna was truly surprised. It had been ages since she was at a family gathering. This was one thing that Tianna desired—to have Gracie reconnected with the family on such a level that made her always embrace and develop a renewed appreciation for family gatherings.

"I guess Irma blew you here with her great strength," she joked as she hugged her little sister, then her husband and their children.

"Surprise!" said about ten church members individually as they gathered at the door. Tianna was truly happy to see each one of them, but grew even more concerned, as family gatherings only included family members. Yet there was no time to dwell on this confusing issue because of all the hugging.

However, when Joshua's brother and his wife, Shadè, entered immediately following the church members, Tianna could not help but feel totally overwhelmed, as if there was something going on that she had no clue about.

"What is going on?" she blurted out as she hugged Shadè's husband. Then she hugged Shadè, and the two complimented each other on their outfits.

Music started to play. Tianna stopped in her tracks.

"Wait a minute! That's—" She stopped speaking.

"I Wanna Know" by Joe was playing. It was a song that she really loved but revealed that to Joshua only, because in her mind, that was not something you let church folks know. They are certainly too sanctimonious to appreciate love songs. The question was, why was it playing here and now?

When the lyrics of the song started, Joshua appeared at the door, lip-synching. "It's amazing how you knock me off my feet, yeah. Every time you come around me I feel weak. Nobody ever made me feel this way. You kiss my lips and then you take my breath away."

Tianna could not believe her eyes and ears. She just stood there, frozen in place, looking at Joshua. She could not recall ever feeling so incapacitated in her life.

The music softened, and Joshua stood in front of her. By this time, her forehead had more ripples than the ocean.

"From the day I laid eyes on you at that little house, I had eyes for no other. Irma brought us together, and I would like it to be forever. So in front of all these witnesses, I want to know . . ." He paused, pulled a small box from his back pocket, went down on one knee, and opened the box.

Tianna put her hands over her mouth.

"Tianna Corrington, will you marry me?"

She turned her back to him with her face in her hand and started to cry. "Oh my goodness," she muttered. "I don't believe you people."

Lee's wife rushed to get her a sheet of paper towel.

"He's waiting!" a voice from the crowd interrupted the silence. It sounded like her mom. She was not sure who it was as at the moment everything just felt so disconcerting.

Tianna wiped her face and turned around. She took a deep breath and paused.

"So will you?" another voice said from the crowd.

"Yes, Joshua Payne, I will marry you," she finally said.

The room was then filled with loud cheers and applause.

Joshua put the ring on her finger, rose to his feet, and lifted her off the ground. She embraced him, and they kissed.

He then held her away from him and looked deeply into her eyes.

"Thank you, Tit-tie," he said with a mischievous grin.

"You're welcome, Joshi-pooh," she responded with a laugh.

Joshua's face immediately changed to an ocean of rippling waves.

"Where did you get that?"

"Ask Ms. Jenny."

"My mom? I can't believe her."

"She told me not to say anything. Please don't sell me out," she said with a sheepish look.

He gave her a half smile and kissed her on her forehead.

"I love you, Tia."

"I loved you too, Joshua."

They kissed again.

Everyone applauded, and the party started.

ABOUT THE AUTHOR

Maureen A. Peters was born and raised on Tortola in the British Virgin Islands, an island located in the Caribbean region. In this debut novel, she captures the dramatic experience of living through a very devastating natural disaster, and finding love in the midst of the storm.

Having had what can be considered a stormy life, Maureen is a strong believer that good can always be found in the midst of any stormy situation.

In the wake of Hurricane Irma, Maureen feels that there are a lot of lessons, many of which were incorporated in the book.

It is her hope that readers will garner an appreciation for life, and that they would make an intentional effort every day to love and care for others.

This book aims to provide encouragement to the people of the British and US Virgin Islands, Puerto Rico, and the other Caribbean Islands that were severely impacted by Hurricanes Irma and Maria. Rebuild we must!

She is the mother of an adult son. They continue to enjoy a life of sun, sea, and surf on the recovering island of Tortola.

Lightning Source UK Ltd.
Milton Keynes UK
UKHW040632100521
383461UK00001B/123